FORENSIC SCIENCE
GLOSSARY

John C. Brenner

CRC Press

Boca R̶a̶t̶o̶n̶ ... gton, D.C.

Library of Congress Cataloging-in-Publication Data

Catalog record is available from the Library of Congress.

Preface

The field of Forensic Science has grown tremendously in the last few decades. With the introduction of advanced procedures and methods of analysis, many new terms and words have emerged. Therefore, in order to communicate more effectively with the layperson and the scientist alike, an understanding of these terms is essential.

It is easy to communicate with an individual when you both work in the same scientific field. The challenge is to explain your laboratory results to people who know little, if nothing, about forensics and may even have only a rudimentary knowledge of chemistry. This book will define both common and unfamiliar forensic terms, and will broaden your knowledge of the language spoken in the forensic environment.

The field of forensics is a very diverse, interesting, exciting, and sometimes confusing science. Most fields of forensics have one or two good reference books that defines the words used in that field. The objective of this book is to combine word definitions from the various fields, into one single source — the *Forensic Science Glossary*. This book will provide an excellent addition to the reference library of those individuals who deal in criminal law, criminal investigation, and those interested in becoming involved in the field of forensics.

This first edition of *Forensic Science Glossary* is by no means inclusive of every forensic term; however, the most common words and terms used in the forensic community may be found and will assist you in understanding the results of laboratory reports, in reading articles, or in conversation with forensic scientists.

John C. Brenner
Albany, New York

Introduction

This Glossary contains terms commonly used in the field of Forensic Science. The definitions provided relate to their use in a forensic context only. These terms come from a variety of related disciplines such as toxicology, drug chemistry, criminalistics, arson investigation, questioned document examination, photography, DNA analysis, and firearms, toolmarks, and fingerprint identification. Each of these areas has their own language and terms and there are excellent reference books specific to each discipline. This Glossary has drawn hundreds of terms from within these various fields into one convenient reference pocketbook of the most commonly used terms.

It is the hope of the author that the *Forensic Science Glossary* will become a tool to help individuals in the non-scientific community, such as court reporters, attorneys, law enforcement personnel, and students who desire to pursue a career in the field, to better understand the terms they come into contact with in the course of their daily work. Laboratory reports of ongoing criminal investigations are only useful to the lawyer or investigator if they can interpret the results.

All of the terms have been included in good faith and every reasonable attempt has been made to confirm definitions, and in the case of commercial terms, to verify the manufacturer. Whenever appropriate, the use of ™ or ® has been included following the name of the entry, although a term may be a registered trademark even if it does not include either symbol. It is also possible that some of the entries listed as "trademarks" may not be registered or properly used by the manufacturers

A listing of firearm manufacturers and their addresses appear in the Appendix. It is possible that some addresses and telephone numbers have changed in view of the recent changes in telephone area codes in many parts of the country.

From the hundreds of current firearms manufacturers, only those whose products are most frequently encountered in the forensic field, such as Colt 45, the derringer, and the .38 Harrington & Richardson revolver, have been included in the Appendix.

If you are aware of any changes or additions that should be included in subsequent editions of the Forensic Science Glossary, please send them to John C. Brenner, 4 Linda Lane, Schenectady, New York, 12303-4920.

About the Author

John C. Brenner has been active in the Forensic Science field for more than 15 years.

His interest in forensic science began in the 1970s, with "Quincy," a popular television program starring Jack Klugman. The show portrayed Klugman as Dr. Quincy, a forensic medical examiner who analyzed physical evidence to recreate the crime, and at the show's conclusion, solved the "crime of the week." Developing profiles of individuals involved in crimes through analysis of the physical evidence intrigued the young John Brenner and served as an impetus for him to seek a career in the Forensic Science field.

He began his formal study in laboratory science in the U.S. Navy as a clinical laboratory worker. While in the Navy, he received his B.Sc. in Health Care Administration from Southern Illinois University. He continued working in the clinical laboratory field after his honorable discharge from the Navy in 1981. Mr. Brenner subsequently received his M.S. in Forensic Science in 1984 from the University of New Haven in West Haven, Connecticut.

Upon completion of his graduate studies in Forensic Science, Mr. Brenner secured a position with a major state police forensic laboratory. He began his career in the Toxicology section and later transferred to the Serology section. Over the next several years, the Serology section expanded to include DNA analysis and was renamed the Bioscience section.

The field of Forensic Science now plays a greater role than ever, both in the investigation of crimes and in the courtroom. His current position has allowed him to give valuable information to investigators by helping to identify and strengthen clues in ongoing investigations. He has also been called upon to give expert witness testimony in more than 130 criminal cases.

A

A   Single-letter designation of the purine base adenine.

AAFS   American Academy of Forensic Sciences. The oversight body for certification of Criminalists.

ABC   American Board of Criminalistics.

absorbance   The measure of concentration of material present; the negative log (base 10) of transmittance [-log 1/T] of product of extinction coefficient, pathlength, and concentration, written as A = Ebc

absorption   A mechanical phenomenon wherein one substance penetrates into the inner structure of another, as in absorbent cotton or a sponge. An optical phenomenon wherein atoms or molecules block or attenuate the transmission of a beam of electromagnetic radiation.

absorption band   A region of the absorption spectrum in which the absorbance passes through a maximum.

absorption elution   An improved, direct way of showing the presence of agglutinogens. In this method, antigenic material is first allowed to come in contact with antisera. The homologous antibody is specifically absorbed by a given agglutinogen.

absorption inhibition   A classical, indirect way of demonstrating the presence of an agglutinogen. This method involves the addition of a titered antiserum to the bloodstain.

absorption spectrum   A plot, or other representation of absorbance, or any function of absorbance, against wavelength, or any function of wavelength.

absorptivity (a)   Absorbance divided by the product of the sample pathlength (b) and the concentration of the absorbing substance (c); a = A/bc.

accelerant   Any material used to initiate or promote the spread of a fire. The most common accelerants are flammable or combustible fluids. Whether a substance is an accelerant depends not on its chemical structure, but on its use. An accelerant may be a solid, liquid, or in some instances, a gas.

accuracy   A measure of the closeness of a test result to the absolute value.

acetaldehyde CH_3CHO. A colorless liquid having a pungent and fruity odor; highly flammable and toxic used chiefly to manufacture acetic acid. Also known as *ethanol*.

acetate   A salt or ester of acetic acid. A manufactured fiber in which the fiber-forming substance is cellulose acetate. Where not less than 92% of the hydroxyl groups are acetylated, the term triacetate may be used as a generic description of the fiber.

acetic acid   A colorless, pungent, mobile liquid, usually obtained by the destructive distillation of wood or by the oxidation of alcohol with ferments. Chemical reagent used in Griess (Walker) test for gunpowder residue detection. Acetic acid forms nitrous acid in reacting with nitrites in gunpowder residue.

acetone   The simplest ketone. A solvent for gunpowder. A highly flammable, water-soluble solvent.

ACES™   *See* Advanced Chemiluminescent Enhancement System.

acid phosphatase   An enzyme which is found in high concentration in seminal fluid. Any nonspecific phosphatase requiring an acid medium for optimum activity.

acid phosphatase test   One of the best known and most widely employed techniques for semen identification. This enzyme can be found in the male prostate gland and is sometimes abbreviated as "AP."

acquired antigen   Antigen not genetically determined and sometimes transient.

activation   The heating of the adsorbent layer on a plate to dry out the moisture and maximize its attraction and retention power.

acrylamide monomer   Produced by the reduction of acrylonitrile by either liquid ammonia or by calcium bisulfite.

acrylic fiber   Generic name for a manufactured fiber in which the fiber-forming substance is any long chain synthetic polymer composed of at least 85% by weight of acrylonitrile units.

actuator   **1.** Part of the firing mechanism in certain automatic firearms which slides forward and back in preparing each cartridge to be fired. Also called *trigger actuator.* **2.** A manually or mechanically operated component which transmits a certain action or energy to other components which are dependent upon movement of the actuator in order to function.

ADA (adenosine deaminase)   An enzyme found in the serum of blood.

addiction   Implies a very severe form of dependence, one involving an overwhelming compulsion for the use of a particular drug.

adenine   A nucleic acid consisting of a chemically linked sequence of subunits. Each subunit contains a nitrogenous base, a pentose sugar, and a phosphate group. One of the four building blocks of DNA.

adenosine triphosphate (ATP)   A nucleoside triphosphate that upon hydrolysis results in energy availability for processes such as muscle contraction and synthesis of marcomolecules, including protein and carbohydrates.

adsorbent   The stationary phase for adsorption thin-layer chromatography. A solid or liquid that adsorbs other substances; e.g., charcoal, silica, metals, water, and mercury.

adsorption   The action of a body, such as charcoal, in condensing and holding a gas or soluble substance upon its surface. The adherence of atoms, ions, or molecules of a gas or liquid to the surface of another substance. Finely divided or microporous materials having a large active surface area are strong adsorbents. The attraction between the surface atoms of a solid and an external molecule by intermolecular forces.

Advanced Chemiluminescent Enhancement System™ (ACES™)   Used for the nonradioactive quantitation of small amounts of human DNA.

AFIS   Automated Fingerprint Identification System.

AFTE   Association of Firearms and Toolmark Examiners.

agar   A polysaccharide extracted from seaweed. A gelatinous product extracted from certain red algae used chiefly as a gelling agent in culture media.

agarose   The neutral gelling fraction of agar commonly used in gel electrophoresis.

agglutination   The clumping together of living cells as a result of a reaction between the cells and an appropriate immune serum.

agglutinin   A chemical product of the process of immunization, arising in blood serum and causing the red corpuscles, with which it is brought into contact, to coalesce into floccules.

agglutinogen   An antigen that stimulates production of a specific antibody (agglutinin) when introduced into an animal body. Outdated term for red-cell antigen.

AK   Adenylate kinase.

albumin   One of a group of heat-coagulable, water-soluble proteins occurring in egg-white, blood serum, milk, and many animal and vegetable tissues.

alcohol   An organic compound having a hydroxyl (-OH) group attached. The lower molecular weight alcohols, methanol (CH_3OH), ethanol (C_2H_5OH), and propanol (C_3H_7OH), are water-soluble.

algorithm   A set of well-defined rules for the solution of a problem in a finite number of steps.

alignment defect   Characters that write improperly in the following respects: a twisted letter, horizontal malalignment, vertical malalignment, or a character "off-its-feet." These defects can be corrected by special adjustments to the typebar and typeblock of a typebar machine.

aliphatic   One of the main groups of hydrocarbons characterized by the straight- or branched-chain arrangement of constituent atoms. Aliphatic hydrocarbons belong to one of three subgroups: (1) alkanes or paraffins, all of which are saturated and comparatively unreactive; (2) the alkenes or alkadiens which are unsaturated (containing double [$C = C$] bonds) and are more reactive; and (3) alkynes, such as acetylene (which contain a triple [$C \equiv C$] bond).

aliquot   A measured amount of liquid taken from the main portion.

alkaline phosphatase   A phosphatase active in alkaline media.

alkaloid   One of a group of nitrogenous organic bases, especially one of vegetable origin, having a powerful toxic effect on animals and man, such as nicotine, cocaine, strychnine, or morphine.

alkanes   An aliphatic hydrocarbon having the chemical formula $C_nH_{2n}+2$. Also known as *paraffin*.

alkyd resin   A class of adhesive resins made from unsaturated acids and glycerol; used as a bonding agent in paints and lacquers.

allele   One of a series of alternative forms of a gene (or VNTR) at a specific locus in a genome. In DNA analysis, the term "alleles" is commonly extended to include DNA fragments of variable length and/or sequence which may have no known transcriptional product but are detected in a polymorphic system.

allele frequency   A measure of the commonness of an allele in a population; the proportion of all alleles of that gene in the population that are of this specific type.

allotypes   Genetically determined polymorphic variants. The term was first introduced to describe the different antigenic forms of rabbit gamma globulins. It was later extended to include polymorphic variants of plasma proteins in general (e.g., haptoglobins, Gc groups) but now includes red cell and white cell polymorphisms.

alloy   A solid of liquid mixture of two or more metals, or of one or more metals with certain nonmetallic elements, as in brass, bronze, or carbon steel.

altered document   A document that contains a change, either as an addition or a deletion.

Alu   A family of repeat DNA sequences, cleaved by the restriction enzyme Alu I, dispersed throughout the genomes of many animal species. The family consists of about 500,000 copies, at 300 bp each, per human genome.

Amadeo Rossi and Co.   A firearms manufacturer.

ambient   Pre-existing or of the normal environment.

amino acid   The building blocks of proteins coded by triplets of bases in DNA blueprint. Any one of a class of organic compounds containing the amino (NH_2) group and the carboxyl (COOH) group.

amitriptyline   A tricyclic antidepressant drug, found to impair skilled performance and to be additive with ethanol in its adverse effects.

ammonia   A colorless gaseous alkaline compound that is very soluble in water, has a characteristic pungent odor, is lighter than air, and is formed as a result of the decomposition of most nitrogenous organic material, such as tissue from dead bodies.

ammoniacal   Pertaining to ammonia or its properties.

amobarbital   A barbiturate derivative, used as a sedative or hypnotic and is available in ampules for intravenous or intramuscular injection for the control of seizures.

amorph   A gene which apparently has no end-product e.g,. a specific antigenic determinant. Sometimes referred to as a 'silent' gene. A mutation that obliterates gene function; a null mutation.

amosite   A monoclinic amphibole form of asbestos having long fibers and a high iron content; used in insulation.

amphetamine   A drug that is representative of a class of structurally related compounds known as phenethylamines. Basis of a group of hallucinogenic, habit-forming drugs which affect the CNS. The sale and use restricted to physicians; trade name Benzedrine.®

amplified fragment length polymorphism (AMP/FLP) Polymerase chain reaction amplified restriction fragment lengths consisting of variable number of tandem repeats.

amplification The production of additional copies of a chromosomal sequence, found as intrachromosomal or extrachromosomal DNA.

amplification blank A control that consists of only amplification reagents without the addition of sample DNA. This control is used to detect DNA contamination of theamplification reagents and material, also known as a *Kit reagent blank.*

amplify To increase the strength or amplitude of extracted DNA material.

amylase An enzyme found in plant and animal tissue which promotes the conversion of starch and glycogen into maltose. In forensics, the Phadebas test is used to detect the enzyme amylase which is found in saliva.

anemia A condition in which the blood is deficient either in quantity or in quality.

analgesic Any drugs, such as salicylates, morphine, or opiates used primarily for the relief of pain.

analysis The determination of the composition of a substance.

analytical The branch of chemistry dealing with techniques which yield any type of information.

analytical gel A gel that consists of all the digested DNA evidence and control DNA samples for a particular forensic case.

angle of impact The internal angle at which blood strikes a target surface relative to the horizontal plane of that target surface. Thus, a straight-on impact would have an impact angle of 90°.

angle of incidence   The angle of incidence as used here conforms to that used in optics to describe reflection and refraction of light rays. The angle is measured with respect to the normal to the surface, rather than to the surface itself. The normal is an imaginary line perpendicular (90°) to the plane of the surface. Thus, a straight-on impact (along the normal) is said to have an angle of incidence of zero.

anidex   A manufactured fiber in which the fiber-forming substance is any long-chain synthetic polymer composed of at least 50% by weight of one or more esters of a monohydric alcohol and acrylic acid.

aniline ink   A fast-drying printing ink that is a solution of a coal tar dye in an organic solvent or a solution of a pigment in an organic solvent or water.

anisotropic   Having different properties in different directions, i.e., when a fibrous substance conducts heat more rapidly along its fibers than across them. Exhibiting double refraction, as a lens or mineral. An object which has properties that differ according to the direction of measurement when viewed in polarized light.

anneal   The formation of double strands from two complementary single strands of DNA and/or RNA. In the second step of each PCR cycle, primers bind or anneal to the 3' end of the target sequence.

annealing   The pairing of complementary single strands of DNA to form a double helix.

anode   In an electrolytic cell, the electrode at which oxidation occurs; the positive terminal of an electrolytic cell.

anonymous loci Specific sites on a chromosome where the gene functions have not been identified.

anthophyllite A natural magnesium–iron silicate; a variety of asbestos occurring as lamellae, radiations, fibers or massive in metamorphic rocks. Also known as *bidalotite*.

antibody A protein produced for body defense in response to an antigen. An antibody is a substance which appears in the plasma or body fluids as a result of stimulation by an antigen and which will react specifically with that antigen in some observable way.

anticoagulant A substance, such as EDTA, which prevents coagulation or clotting of the blood.

antidepressant A drug, such as imipramine and tranylcypromine, that relieves depression by increasing central sympathetic activity.

antigen A foreign substance, usually a protein, capable of stimulating an antibody response for body defense. Any substance which, when introduced parenterally into an individual lacking the substance, stimulates the production of an antibody that, when mixed with the antibody, reacts with it in some observable way.

antigenic determinant The particular site on an antigen molecule which combines with the corresponding antibody.

antigenicity Potency as an antigen.

anti-human globulin (Coombs reagent). An antibody produced in an animal (usually a rabbit) in response to the injection of human globulin.

antiparallel A term used to describe the opposite orientations of the two strands of a DNA double helix; the 5′ end of one strand aligns with the 3′ end of the other strand.

antisera Anti-human sera can be produced by injecting human serum into various animals, such as the horse, goat, sheep, rabbit, duck, hen, or guinea pig.

antiserum Any immune serum that contains antibodies active chiefly in destroying a specific infecting virus or bacterium.

antitoxin A substance found in the blood serum and in other body fluids which is specifically antagonistic to some particular toxin.

anvil marks Microscopic marks impressed on the forward face of the rim of a rimfire cartridge case as it is forced against the breech end of the barrel by the firing pin. These marks are characteristic of the breech under the firing pin and have been used to identify a firearm.

AP Abbreviation for armor-piercing ammunition.

aperture (f/number) Lens opening. The opening in a lens system through which light passes. The size of aperture is either fixed or adjustable. Lens openings are usually calibrated in f-numbers.

aqueous solution A solution with the solvent as water.

aramid A manufactured fiber in which the fiber-forming substance is any long-chain synthetic polyamide in which at least 85% of the amide linkage is attached directly to two aromatic rings.

aromatic An organic compound having as part of its structure a benzene ring. The term "aromatic" as used in the fragrance industry is used to describe essential oils, which are not necessarily in the chemical sense.

arsenic A chemical element (As). A medicinal and poisonous element; a brittle steel-gray hexagonal mineral, the native form of the element.

arson The criminal act of intentionally setting fire to a building or other property.

arterial spurting   Characteristic bloodstain patterns on a target surface resulting from blood exiting under pressure from a breached artery. These patterns are characterized by their specific appearance and shape.

asbestos   A white or light-gray mineral, obtained chiefly from actinolite and amphibole, occurring in long slender needles or fibrous masses which may be woven or shaped into acid-resisting, non-conducting, and fireproof articles.

ASCLD   American Society of Crime Laboratory Directors.

asepsis   The state of being free from pathogenic microorganisms.

atom   The smallest unit of an element which still retains the chemical characteristics of that element. An atom is made up of protons and neutrons in a nucleus surrounded by electrons. A molecule of water (H_2O) consists of two atoms of hydrogen and one atom of oxygen.

atomic absorption (AA)   A method of qualitative and quantitative elements analysis where the element which is being analyzed must be dissociated from its chemical bonds after which the atoms of this element will absorb radiation of an energy specific for that element. The amount of energy absorbed is proportional to the concentration of that element in the specimen. Atomic absorption has applications in many fields of science. Its main application in forensic science is to analyze cotton swabs for some of the elements in primer residue.

atomize   To break into discrete atoms, usually by the application of extreme heat, as in atomic absorption. To break a liquid into tiny droplets, as occurs in fuel-injected engines or in the production of aerosol sprays.

attenuated total reflection (ATR)   Reflection that occurs when an absorbing coupling mechanism acts in the process of total internal reflection to make the reflectance less than unity.

attenuation   An adjustment of the signal amplifier response which results in the reduction of the electronic signal.

atypical antibody   An antibody which occurs as an irregular feature of the serum, e.g., anti-D.

auto-antibody   An antibody which reacts with the red cells of the individual in whose serum it is found. It usually reacts upon the red cells of most other individuals as well.

autoclave   An airtight vessel for heating and sometimes agitating its contents under high steam pressure; used for industrial processing, sterilizing, and cooking with moist or dry heat at high temperatures.

autopsy   A postmortem examination of the body to determine cause of death.

autoradiogram (autoradiograph)   The resultant X-ray film following exposure to a radioactive source. A DNA probe tagged with a radioactive isotope such as ^{32}P (radioactive phosphorus) will expose an X-ray film where the probe hybridizes to complementary sequences on the blot in contact with the film.

automatic action   A firearm design that feeds cartridges, fires, and ejects cartridge cases as long as the trigger is fully depressed and there are cartridges available in the feed system.

autorad   An X-ray film of the hybridization between the radioactive probe and the complementary exposed strand of DNA.

autoradiography   A technique for detecting radioactivity in a specimen by producing an image on a photographic film or plate.

auto safety   A locking device on some firearms designed to return to the "ON" ("SAFE") position when the firearm is opened.

autosome   Non-sex chromosome. There are 22 autosomes in the human genome.

axillary   Attached to a joint.

azeotrope   A mixture of two or more compounds which has a constant boiling point. The composition of the vapor above the azeotropic mixture has the same relative concentrations of compounds as does the boiling liquid. Azeotropic mixtures cannot be separated by fractional distillation.

azlon   Any textile fiber derived from protein, such as casein.

azo dye   A result of the Griess test where nitrites from gunpowder residues are converted to an orange-red dye.

B

BAC   Blood alcohol content.

background   Apparent absorption caused by anything other than the substance for which the analysis is being made.

background discrimination   The ability of a measuring instrument, circuit, or other device to distinguish signals from background noise.

background radiation   Radiation from a source other than the test sample specifically being analyzed.

backspatter   Blood that is directed back towards its source of energy. Backspatter is often associated with gunshot wounds of entrance.

bacterial DNA   The DNA found in bacteria.

ball-point pen   A writing instrument having as its marking tip a small, freely rotating ball bearing that rolls the ink onto the paper. Many of these pens use a highly viscous, nonaqueous ink, but in recent years construction of some pens has been adapted to use water-based inks.

ballistics   The study of a projectile in motion. Often confused with *firearms identification.*

band   A radioactive signal on an autorad usually caused by a fragment of human or bacterial DNA that combines with a radiolabeled DNA probe.

band-shifting   The phenomenon where DNA fragments in one lane of an electrophoresis gel migrate across the gel more rapidly than identical fragments in a second lane.

barbiturate A derivative of barbituric acid which produces depression of the central nervous system and consequent sedation.

Barr bodies A condensed, inactivated X-chromosome inside the nuclear membrane in interphase somatic cells of women.

barrel That part of a firearm through which a projectile or shot charge travels under the impetus of powder gases, compressed air, or other like means; may be rifled or smooth.

barrier filter A filter used in fluorescence microscopy that suppresses unnecessary excitation light that has not been absorbed by the fiber and selectively transmits only the fluorescence.

baseline The ruled or imaginary line upon which the writing rests.

baselining Adjusting the baselines of detected dye colors to the same level for a better comparison of relative signal intensity.

bases The chemical units (adenine, thymine, guanine, and cytosine) whose order in DNA molecules governs the genetic code.

base pair (bp) A partnership of A with T or of C with G found in a DNA double helix.

base sequence The order of bases in a DNA molecule.

Becke line The bright halo near the boundary of a fiber that moves with respect to that boundary as the microscope is focused through best focus.

Becke line method A method for determining the refractive index of a fiber relative to its mountant by noting the direction in which the Becke line moves when the focus is changed. The Becke line will always move toward the higher refractive index medium (fiber or mountant) when focus is raised and will move toward the lower refractive index medium when focus is lowered. Is a traditional means for matching a particle with an immersion liquid.

benzene   A hexagonal organic molecule having a carbon atom at each point of the hexagon, and a hydrogen atom attached to each carbon atom. Molecules which contain a benzene ring are known as aromatic.

benzidine   A grayish-yellow, white or reddish gray crystalline powder; its an organic synthesis, manufacture of dyes especially of Congo red. Also used for the detection of blood stainand as a stiffening agent in rubber compounding.

benzoylecognine   A cocaine metabolite.

Beretta   A handgun manufacturer.

between-the-lens shutter/lens shutter   A shutter whose blades operate between two elements of the lens.

bin or binning   A conservative method of calculating population frequency by combining groups of fragment sizes into defined groups instead of making calculations from a single fragment size.

biological sample bag (Biobag)   collection of biological stains, acquired from physical evidence, sealed in a plastic bag.

biopsy   A small piece of tissue excised for the purpose of analysis.

bipod   A two-legged rest or stand, as for a rifle or machine gun.

birefringence   The splitting of a light beam into two components, which travel at different velocities, by a material. The numerical difference in refractive indices for a fiber, given by the formula: $\bar{a}n\bar{a}-nZ\bar{a}$. Birefringence can be calculated by determining the retardation (r) and thickness (T) at a particular point in a fiber and by using the formula: B = r (nm)/1000T (_m).

black powder   The earliest form of propellant. It is a mechanical mixture of potassium nitrate or sodium nitrate, charcoal, and sulfur.

"blank" paper   A sheet of paper that contains no visible or readily visible writing. At times a 'blank' paper may contain impressed or latent writing that can be made legible with proper treatment.

blood group   An immunologically distinct, genetically determined class of human erythrocyte antigens, identified as A, B, AB, and O. A classification of red blood cell surface antigens, for example ABO.

bloodstain   Blood that has come in contact with a surface.

bolt action   A firearm in which the breech closure is in line with the bore at all times. It is manually reciprocated to load, unload, and cock and is locked in placed by breech-bolt lugs and engaging abutments usually in the receiver.

bore   The interior of a barrel forward of the chamber.

bore brush   A brush usually having brass of plastic bristles which is used to clean deposits from the bore of a firearm.

bore diameter   **1.** In a rifled barrel it is the minor diameter of a barrel which is the diameter of a circle formed by the tops of the lands. **2.** In a shotgun it is the interior dimensions of the barrel forward of the chamber, but before the choke.

bounce lighting   Flash or tungsten light bounced off the ceiling or walls in order to give the effect of natural or available light.

bovine albumin   Any one of a class of protein substances found in the blood of a bovine animal. Also known as *bovine albumin serum (BSA)*.

bp   An abbreviation for base pairs; distance along DNA is measured in bp.

"brass"   A slang term sometimes used for fired cartridge cases.

breech   The part of a firearm at the rear of the bore into which the cartridge of propellant is inserted.

breech block   The locking and cartridge head supporting mechanism of a firearm that does not operate in line with the axis of the bore.

breech blot   The locking and cartridge head supporting mechanism of a firearm that operates in line with the axis of the bore.

breech face   That part of the breech block or breech bolt which is against the head of the cartridge case or shotshell during firing.

breech-face markings   Negative impression of the breech face of the firearm found on the head of the cartridge case after firing.

Brentamine Fast Salt Blue B   A chemical used for the detection of acid phosphatase. Acid phosphatase is an enzyme, found in high concentrations in seminal fluid. The presence of acid phosphatase only indicates the presence of semen.

broad heritability (H2)   The proportion of total phenotypic variance at the population level that is contributed by genetic variance.

Browning Arms Co.   A firearms manufacturer.

BTU (British thermal unit)   The amount of heat energy required to raise the temperature of one pound of water by 1°F. One BTU equals 252 calories.

buccal cells   Cells derived from the inner cheek lining. These cells are present in the saliva or can be gently scraped from the inner cheek surface.

buffer   Solutions that tend to resist changes in their pH as acid or base is added.

buffy coat   The whitish layer of cells (white blood cells plus platelets) overlaying the red cell pellet after centrifugation of whole blood.

bullet-bearing surface   That part of the outer surface of a bullet that comes into direct contact with the interior surface of the barrel.

bullet   A non-spherical projectile for use in a rifled barrel.

bullet, capped   A standard lead bullet having a harder metal jacket over the nose. Also known as *metal-point bullet.*

bullet creep   The movement of a bullet out of the cartridge case due to the recoil of the firearm and the inertia of the bullet. Also called *bullet starting.* Also known as *popping.*

bullet, frangible   A projectile designed to disintegrate upon impact on a hard surface in order to minimize ricochet or spatter.

bullet jacket   A usually metallic cover over the core.

bullet recovery system   Any method which will allow the undamaged recovery of a fired bullet. Water tanks and cotton boxes are most commonly in use.

bullet types   Plain lead or coated.

bullet wipe   The discolored area on the immediate periphery of a bullet hole, caused by bullet lubricant, lead, smoke, bore debris, or possibly, jacket material. Sometimes called *burnishing* or *leaded edge*.

burning   Normal combustion in which the oxidant is molecular oxygen.

burning rate   The rate at which combustion proceeds across a fuel.

burr striations   A roughness or rough edge, especially one left on metal in casting or cutting. A tool or device that raises a burr.

butabarbital   A short- to intermediate-acting barbiturate derivative.

butalbital   An occasionally encountered short-acting barbiturate closely related to Talbutal and less closely to Amobarbital and Secobarbital. Intoxication can result in lethargy, confusion, disorientation, and ataxia.

butane   A fuel gas having the formula C_4H_{10}. A constituent of LP gas.

butt   In handguns, the bottom part of the grip and/or grip frame. In long guns, the rear of shoulder end of the stock.

C

C   A single-letter designation of the pyrimidine base cytosine.

caliber   In **firearms** it is the approximate diameter of the circle formed by the tops of the lands of a rifled barrel. In **ammunition** it is a numerical term, without the decimal point, included in a cartridge name to indicate a rough approximation of the bullet diameter.

calibrate   To determine, by measurement or comparison with a standard, the correct value of each scale reading on a meter or other device, or the correct value for each setting of a control knob.

calibration   Determining the response of some analytical method to known amounts of pure analyte.

calorie   The amount of energy required to raise the temperature of one gram of water by 1°C.

cannabidiol   A constituent of cannabis which upon isomerization to a tetrahydrocannabinol has some of the physiologic activity of marijuana.

cannabinol $C_{21}H_{26}O_2$ A physiologically inactive phenol formed by spontaneous dehydrogenation of tetrahydrocannabinol from cannabis.

Cannabis   A genus of tall annual herbs in the family Cannabaceae having erect stems, with 3 to 7 elongated leaflets and pistillate flowers in spikes along the stem.

cannelure   A circumferential groove generally of a knurled or plain appearance in a bullet or cartridge case.

Three uses include crimping, lubrication, and identification.

capillary   A narrow-bore glass tube. Capillary column gas chromatography employs glass tubes having an inside diameter of approximately .2 to .5 millimeters and a length of 3 to 300 meters. The walls of a capillary column are coated with an adsorbent or adsorbents medium (a liquid phase in which the sample dissolves).

carbine   A rifle of short length and light weight originally designed for mounted troops.

carbon   The element upon which all organic molecules are based.

carbon copy   A copy of a typewritten document made by means of carbon paper. An exact replica; duplicate.

carbon dioxide   A molecule consisting of one atom of carbon and two atoms of oxygen which is a major combustion product of the burning of organic materials. Carbon dioxide (CO_2) is the result of complete combustion of carbon.

carbon impression   Any typewriting placed on the paper by the action of the typeface striking through carbon paper. Generally, carbon impressions are "carbon copies," but sometimes original typewriting is made directly through a carbon paper or carbon film ribbon.

carbon ink (India ink)   One of the oldest forms of writing ink; commonly referred to as India ink even though the ink was first used in China. In its simplest form carbon ink consists of amorphous carbon shaped into a solid cake with glue. It is converted into a liquid for writing by grinding the cake and suspending the particles in a water–glue medium. Occasionally, a pigmented dye is added to improve the color.

carbon monoxide (CO)   A colorless, odorless, very toxic gas, formed by burning carbon or organic fuels. A gaseous molecule having the formula CO, which is the product of incomplete combustion of organic materials. Carbon monoxide has an affinity for hemoglobin that is approximately 200 times stronger than that of oxygen. It is highly poisonous.

carbonic anhydrase II (CA II)   An enzyme present in erythrocytes which catalyses the formation of carbonic acid by water and carbon dioxide, and also the decomposition of carbonic acid.

carrier   An individual with only one of two possible copies of an abnormal gene. The heterozygous state. An individual who possesses a mutant allele but does not express it in the phenotype because of a dominant allelic partner; thus, an individual of genotype **Aa** is a carrier of **a** if there is complete dominance of **A** over **a**.

cartridge   A single unit of ammunition consisting of the case, primer and propellant with or without one or more projectiles. Also applies to a shotshell.

cartridge case   The container for all the other components which comprise a cartridge.

cassette film holder   A light-proof holder used in autoradiography for exposing X-ray film to radioactive blots.

cast-off pattern   Blood that has been projected onto a surface from other than an impact site. This pattern is produced when blood is thrown from a bloody object in motion.

catalyst   A substance that increases the rate of chemical reaction without undergoing a permanent change in its structure.

cathode   The electrode at which reduction takes place in an electrochemical cell.

cation   A positively charged atom, or group of atoms, or a radical which moves to the negative pole (cathode) during electrolysis.

Caucasian   A member of the white-skinned division of the human race.

Caucasoid   Of or pertaining to the so-called "white race," characterized by skin color ranging from very white to dark brown; a member of this ethic group; a Caucasian.

CDM   Criterion Die and Machine Company. A firearms manufacturer.

ceiling principle   A highly conservative method of calculating allele frequencies in populations by stating that any frequency below 10% must be reported as 10%. Its purpose is to eliminate bias based upon ethnic subgroups.

cell division   The process whereby a mother cell gives rise to two identical daughter cells (mitosis) or four gametes (meiosis).

cellulose acetate gel   A support medium through which charged molecules are moved by electrophoresis.

cellulosic fiber   Fiber composed of polymer formed from glucose.

centrifuge   A rotating device for separating liquids of different specific gravities or for separating suspended colloidal particles, such as clay particles in an aqueous suspension, according to particle-size fractions by centrifugal force.

certification   The recognition of a particular level of professional qualifications. A national organization, the American Board of Forensic Document Examiners, Inc., has set up a certification program for document examiners based upon a review and testing of their qualifications. This nationwide program, established in 1978, will provide a register of well-qualified document examiners.

chain reaction   A self-propagating chemical reaction in which activation on one molecule leads successfully to activation of many others. Combustion reaction are of this kind.

chamber   The rear part of the barrel bore that has been formed to accept a specific cartridge. Revolver cylinders are multi-chambered. A glass chamber in which Thin-layer chromatography development is carried out.

chamber marks   Individual microscopic marks placed upon a cartridge case by the chamber wall as a result of any or all of the following: (1) chambering, (2) expansion during firing, and (3) extraction.

character   Some attribute of an individual within a species for which various heritable differences can be defined.

characteristics Any property or mark that distinguishes and in document examination commonly refers to identifying details. There are two groups of characteristics—class and individual.

charred document   A document that has become blackened and brittle through burning or through exposure to excessive heat.

Charter Arms   A firearms manufacturer.

checkering   To mark with squares or crossed lines.

Chelex®   A chelating resin that has a high affinity for polyvalent metal ions. It is composed of stytrene divinylbenzene copolymers containing paired iminodiacetate ions which act as chelatin groups.

chemical change   Rearrangement of the atoms, ions, or radicals of one or more substances, resulting in the formation of new substance, often having entirely different properties. Also known as a *chemical reaction*.

chemiluminescence   Non-radioactive method for DNA analysis, using VNTR probes are tagged with alkaline phosphatase, which reacts with a detection reagent to generate light. The light produces an image on X-ray film.

chemistry   A basic science concerned with (1) the structure and behavior of atoms (elements); (2) the composition and properties of compounds; (3) the reactions that occur between substances and the resultant energy exchange; and (4) the laws that unite these phenomena into a comprehensive system.

chimera   An organism whose cells derive from two or more distinct zygote lineages, e.g., the vascular anastomoses which may occur between twins (a twin of genetic type O may have a bone marrow implantation from its twin of group A. Throughout life therefore he has a major red cell population of group O and a minor population of red cells of group A).

chi-square test (χ^2)   A statistical test to determine how closely an observed set of data values correspond to the values expected, under a specific hypothesis.

chlordiazepoxide hydrochloride   Crystals, toxic in high concentrations. Central nervous system depressant.

chloroform   Once used as an anesthetic. Chloroform undergoes considerable biotransformation in man, with the formation of carbon dioxide and hydrochloric acid.

choke/shotgun   An interior constriction at or near the muzzle end of a shotgun barrel bore for the purpose of controlling shot dispersion.

choline   A crystalline base found in plants and animals, a constituent of lecithin and certain other lipids.

chromatid   One of the two attached daughter strands or "chromosomes" of a mother chromosome observable during mitosis of meiosis.

chromatin   The complex of DNA and protein in the nucleus of the interphase cell. Individual chromosomes cannot be distinguished in it. It was originally recognized by its reaction with stains specific for DNA.

chromatogram   The complete array of distinctively colored bands produced by chromatography. A series of peaks and valleys printed or written on a paper chart where each peak represents a component or mixture of two or more unresolved components in a mixture separated by gas or liquid chromatography.

chromatography   A method for the separation and analysis of small quantities of substances by passing a solution through a column of finely divided powder which selectively adsorbs the constituents in one or more sharply defined, often colored bands.

chromogen   Any organic coloring matter or substance capable of yielding a dye.

chromosome   A nuclear structure in eukaryotes that carries a portion of the genome. The human has 46 chromosomes per nucleus; 22 homologous pairs of autosomes and 2 sex chromosomes.

chromosome theory of inheritance   The unifying theory stating that inheritance patterns may be generally explained by assuming that genes are located in specific sites on chromosomes.

chronograph   An instrument for recording graphically the moment or duration of an event, measuring intervals of time.

chrysotile A fibrous form of serpentine that constitutes one type of asbestos.

CIL (Canadian Industries Ltd.) Imperial/Canuck. A firearms and ammunition manufacturer.

citrate Formed in the citrate synthase reaction from oxaloacetate and acetyl-CoA.

class A group of items which share common properties or characteristics.

class characteristic Not all characteristics encountered in document examination are peculiar to a single person or thing, and one that is common to a group may be described as a class characteristic. Traits that define a group of items collectively.

Clerke Clerke Technicorp. A firearms manufacturer.

clip A separate cartridge container used to rapidly reload the magazine of a firearm. Sometimes improperly used to describe removable magazines. Also called *stripper.*

clogged (dirty) typeface Over prolonged use, the typeface becomes filled with lint, dirt, and ink, particularly in letters with closed loops, such as o, e, p, and g. If this condition is allowed to continue without cleaning, the printed impression will actually print with the clogged areas shaded or solid black.

clone Describes a large number of cells or molecules identical with a single ancestral cell or molecule.

cloned DNA A DNA sequence ligated into a vector and replicated as the vector replicates in its host.

cloning vector A plasmid or phage that is used to 'carry' inserted foreign DNA for the purposes of producing more material or a protein product.

clot   A blood clot is formed by a complex mechanism involving plasma protein fibrinogens, platelets, and other clotting factors. It is observed as a network of fibrous material (fibrin and red blood cells). Subsequently, the blood clot begins to retract, causing a separation of the remaining liquid portion which in now referred to as serum.

cloth ribbon   A type of ribbon use in some models of typewriters.

cobaltous chloride   Used in absorbent for ammonia, electroplating, sympathetic inks, in soil and animal feeds and vitamin B-12.

cocaine   A colorless to white crystalline powder. Used as a local anesthetic (medicine or dentistry), usually as the hydrochloride. Also called coke, snow, or freebase.

codeine   A narcotic alkaloid. Used in medicine and cough syrups, highly toxic and habit-forming narcotic.

codon   A sequence of three bases on the DNA molecule, that represents an amino acid or a termination signal. Groups of codons form genes.

coefficient of form   A numerical term indicating the general profile of a projectile.

coefficient of inbreeding (F)   The proportion of homozygous loci in an individual; or, the probability that both alleles at corresponding loci were inherited from the same ancestor.

coefficient of relationship (r)   The proportion of genes that any two individuals have in common. It is the proportion of the genomes inherited from a common ancestor; or, the probability that two individuals have inherited a specific gene or DNA fragment from a common ancestor.

coefficient of variation (CV)   A statistical measure of dispersion relatin the measure of dispersion (SD) to the average of mean (X). CV = SD X × 100.

collation   As used in this text, critical comparison or side-by-side examination.

collodion   Cellulose nitrate deposited from a solution of 60% ether and 40% alcohol; used for making fibers and film in membranes.

color balance   The ability of a film to reproduce the colors of a scene. Color films are balanced in manufacture for exposure to light of a certain color quality: daylight, tungsten, ect. Color balance also refers to the reproduction of colors in color prints, which can be altered during the printing process.

Colt Firearms   A firearms manufacturer.

combination gun   A multiple-barreled firearm designed to handle different sizes or types of ammunition.

combustion   An exothermic chain reaction between oxidizing and reducing agents, or betweenoxygen and fuel.

comparison   The act of setting two or more items side by side to weigh their identifying qualities. It implies not only a visual but also a mental act in which the elements of one item are related to the counterparts of the other.

comparison microscope   Essentially two microscopes connected to an optical bridge which allows the viewer to observe two objects simultaneously with the same degree of magnification. This instrument can have a monocular or binocular eyepiece. Sometimes referred to as a *comparison microscope.*

compensator   Any variety of optical devices that can be placed in the light path of a polarizing microscope to introduce fixed or variable retardation comparable with that exhibited by the fiber. The retardation and signs of elongation of the fiber may then be determined. Compensators may employ a fixed mineral plate of constant or varying thickness or a mineral plate that may be rotated to alter the thickness presented to the optical path (and retardation introduced) by a set amount.

compensator, full-wave (red plate)   A compensator using a plate of gypsum, selenite, or quartz, which introduces a fixed retardation between 530 to 550 nm (approximately the retardation of the first-order red color on the Michel-Levy chart).

compensator, quarter wave   A compensator, usually with a mica plate, which introduces a fixed retardation between 125 to 150 nm.

compensator, quartz wedge   A wedge, cut from quartz, having continuously variable retardation extending over several orders of interference colors (usually 3 to 7).

compensator, Sénamont   A quarter-wave plate inserted above the specimen in the parallel 0″ position with a rotating calibrated analyzer. Measures low retardation and requires the use of monochromatic light.

compensator, tilting (Berek)   A compensator typically containing a plate of calcite or quartz, which can be rotated by means of a calibrated drum to introduce variable retardation up to about ten orders.

complementary strand of DNA   A strand of DNA that binds to another because its base pair are complementary; e.g., ATTACG which will only combine with TAATGC.

complete digestion   The action of a restriction enzyme in completely cutting the DNA at a specific site.

complexity   The total length of different sequences of DNA present in a given preparation.

component   **1.** One of the elements or compounds present in a system such as a phase, a mixture, a solution, or a suspension in which it may or may not be uniformly dispersed. **2.** A compound or a group of unresolved compounds represented by a peak on a chromatogram.

compound   A chemical combination of two or more elements, or two or more different atoms arranged in the same proportions and in the same structure throughout the substance. A compound is different from a mixture in that the components of a mixture are not chemically bonded together.

conclusion   A scientific conclusion results from relating observed facts by logical, common sense reasoning in accordance with established rules or laws. The document examiner's conclusions are so derived.

concentration   The amount of a substance in a stated unit of a mixture or solution. Common methods of stating concentration are percent by weight, percent by volume, or weight per unit volume.

conduction   Passage of heat from one material to another by direct contact.

conductivity   The ability of a material to transfer energy from one place to another. Thermal conductivity describes a substance's ability to transmit heat. Electrical conductivity describes a substance's ability to transmit electrical current. Conductivity is the opposite of resistivity.

confidence interval   A statistical measure of confidence in a calculated value. A 95% confidence interval equates to the expectation that the value in question will lie within the range stated 95% of the time and outside the range 5%. A certain allele in a population may have a calculated frequency of 1 in 500 people with confidence limits of 1 in 400 to 1 in 600 at the 99% confidence interval.

confidence limits Limits attached to a confidence interval. The 95% confidence limits, for example, when measuring a 10-kb allele on a gel in a certain laboratory may be 9.9 to 10.1 kb.

contact print A print made by exposing photographic paper while it is held tightly against the negative. Images in the print will be the same size as those in the negative.

contrast The density range of a negative, print, or slide; the brightness range of a subject or the scene lighting.

control lane an electrophoresis lane that contains a known sample of DNA.

controls Samples of predetermined concentration (known or unknown to the analyst) treated as unknowns in an assay. Controls are included as part of quality control for each test run.

convection Transfer of heat by the movement of molecules in a gas or liquid, with the less dense fluid rising. The majority of heat transfer in a fire is by convection.

copolymer A mixed polymer, the product of polymerization of at least two substance at the same time.

copper-clad steel A composite structure of copper and steel used for the manufacture of certain bullet jackets.

copy pencil A pencil whose marking substance consists of a mixture of graphite and an aniline dye. When the pencil stroke is moistened the dye develops into a strong purple or in some cases, a blue color. The developed stroke is more difficult to erase than ordinary pencil writing. Some refer to this kind of writing instrument as an indelible pencil.

copybook form The design of letters that is fundamental to a writing system. This term is derived from the old methods of teaching handwriting from a copybook containing engraved script printed on each page for the student to imitate.

core   A fiber or fibers running lengthwise through the center of a cordage.

coronary artery   Either of two arteries arising in the aortic sinuses that supply the heart tissue with blood.

correlation coefficient   A statistical measure of the extent to which variations in one variable are related to variations in another.

corrosion   The degradation of metals or alloys due to reaction with the environment. It is accelerated by acids, bases, or heat.

cortex   The main structural component of hair consisting of elongated and fusiform (spindle-shaped) cells. The cortex may contain pigment grains, air spaces called corticalfusi, and structures called ovoid bodies.

cortical fusi   Variable amounts of delicate air spaces contained within the cortex.

covariance   A statistical measure used in computing the correlation coefficient between two variables; the covariance is the mean of $(x–x)$ $(y–y)$ over all pairs of values for the variables x and y, where x is the mean of the x values and y is the mean of the y values.

course   The row of loops or stitches running across a knit fabric, corresponding to the filling in woven fabrics.

crack   Concentrated form of cocaine which is used in vapor form. It is smoked or inhaled through "crack pipes." It is a highly addictive drug that causes psychotic behavior which is often times violent.

cracking   A refining process involving decomposition and molecular recombination of organic compounds, especially hydrocarbons obtained by distillation of petroleum, by means of heat, to form molecules suitable for various uses such as motor fuels, solvents or plastics. Cracking takes places in the absence of oxygen.

crane/yoke   The part of a solid frame revolver on which the cylinder is swung out to accomplish loading and ejecting.

creatinine   The anhydride of creatine, occurring normally in blood and urine; isolated as white or yellowish prismatic crystals.

crime specimen   A specimen left at the scene of a crime by the perpetrator.

crimp   The waviness of a fiber.

crossbolt   A transverse operating type of lock used on some double barrel firearms.

cross-over marks   Oblique, flattened areas along silk fibers caused by the overlapping of extruded silk fibers before they have dried completely.

crocidolite   A lavender-blue, indigo-blue, or leek-green asbestiform variety of riebeckite. It occurs in fibrous, massive, and earthy forms. Also known as *blue asbestos*; *krokidolite*.

cross-hybridization   The binding of a probe to a DNA sequence other than the intended target sequence. This occurs because of homology between the probe and the sequence and because low-stringency hybridization wash conditions are followed.

cross mark (his mark)   Historically, many who could not write signed with a cross mark or "X." This authenticating mark is still used today by illiterates and if properly witnessed, it can legally stand for a signature.

cross-over   The process by which genetic material is exchanged between homologous chromosomes. It can occur at mitosis or meiosis.

cross-over electrophoresis   The system takes advantage of the electroendosmotic properties of a gel medium to carry out immunoelectrophoretic analysis of an antibody-antigen reaction. Under the influence of electrophoresis, the antigen and the antibody migrate toward each other and a precipitate is formed at the point of their interaction.

cross section   Any specimen, figure, or diagram presenting a representation typical of the whole.

crown   The raised portion of a strand in a twisted cordage.

cupricammonium process   A process for making rayon by dissolving cellulose in an ammoniacal copper solution and reconverting it to cellulose by treatment with acid.

cursive writing; handwriting   Writing in which the letters are for the most part joined together.

cuticle   An outer skin or pellicle; the epidermis. The layer of scales composing the outer surface of a hair shaft. Cuticular scales are normally classified into three basic types; coronal (crown-like), spinous (petal-like), and imbricate (flattened).

cuticular scales   Human hair cuticle is a thin translucent layer surrounding the hair shaft. The layer consists of overlapping, non-nucleated, pigment-free cells which form scales.

cyanoacrylate adhesive   These adhesives have excellent polymerizing and bonding properties. Used in fountain pens, rubber printing plates, optical lens, rubber swimming masks and in radiation-measuring instruments.

cycle   The PCR cycle consists of three steps: (1) denaturation of the template; (2) annealing of primers to complementary sequences at an empirically determined temperature; and (3) extension of the bound primers by a DNA polymerase.

cylinder   The rotatable part of a revolver that contains the chambers.

cylinder alignment   The concentricity of the chamber in a revolver cylinder to the bore of the barrel; the alignment of their axes.

cylinder latch   A device which permits the swinging out of the cylinder from the frame of arevolver.

cystolith   A mineral and usually somewhat crystalline concretion in the epidermal or subjacent cells of the leaf in some plants, especially of the nettle family.

cytogenetics   Area of biology concerned with chromosomes and their implications in genetics.

cytology   The science dealing with structure, functions, and life history of cells.

cytoplasm   Substance of cell-body exclusive of nucleus. Describes the material between the plasma membrane and the nucleus.

D

Damascus barrel   An obsolete barrel-making process. The barrel is formed by twisting or braiding together steel and iron wires or bars. The resulting cable is then wound around a mandrel and forged into a barrel tube. Sometimes called *laminated barrel.*

dark-field microscopy   Descriptive of the appearance of the image of the specimen when this technique is used. Various details of the specimen appear as bright features on a dark field or background. Dark-field microscopy can be used to accentuate refraction images.

data bank   A complete collection of information such as contained in automated files.

database   An empirically derived group of DNA types obtained by DNA typing people of known ethnicity.

decant   The process of pouring off the supernatant during separation from a pellet after a mixture has been centrifuged or left to settle.

decipher   To determine the meaning of, as hieroglyphics or illegible writing. To translate from cipher into ordinary characters. To determine the meaning of (anything obscure).

defecation   The elimination of solid waste matter from the intestines.

defect   Any abnormality or maladjustment in a typewriter that is reflected in its work and leads to its individualization or identification.

deflagrate   To burn with intense heat and light; i.e., gunpowder is said to deflgrate.

degradation   In reference to the quality of the DNA. Degradation is indicated by a smear of DNA fragments on a yield gel. A type of decomposition characteristics of high molecular weight substances such as proteins, and polymers. It may result from oxidation, heat, solvents, bacterial action, or in the case of body proteins from infectious microorganisms.

dehydration   Removal of water from any substance.

deletion   Loss of one or more nucleotides from a DNA strand. This may result in a gene mutation.

delustering   The treatment of synthetic yarns and fabrics by special pigments or other chemicals in order to reduce their natural luster.

delustrant   A substance used to produce dull surfaces on textile fabric; chiefly used are barium sulfate, clays, chalk, titanium dioxide, etc. They are applied in the finishing coat.

delta (fingerprint)   The outer, terminal, point of the pattern, nearest the type line divergence.

denaturation   Describes the conversion of DNA from the double-stranded to the single-stranded state; separation of the strands is most often accomplished by heating. A change in the molecular structure of globular proteins that may be induced by bringing a protein solution to its boiling point, or by exposing it to acid or alkalies or to various detergents.

denatured   A sample of DNA that is single stranded.

denier   A unit of rayon or silk yarn size, based on a standard weight of 5 centigrams per 450 meters of silk.

density   The blackness of an area in a negative or print that determines the amount of light that will pass through it or reflect from it. Density is mass per unit volume (g/cc).

deoxyribonucleic acid (DNA)   The molecule of heredity. DNA is composed of deoxyribonucleic building blocks, each containing a base: adenine (A), thymine (T), cytosine (C), or guanine (G); a deoxyribose sugar (S); and a phosphate group (P).

deoxyribonucleotides   The building blocks of DNA.

depth of field   The distance range between the nearest and farthest objects that appear in acceptably sharp focus in a photograph. Depth of field depends on the lens opening, the focal length of the lens, and the distance from the lens to the subject.

depurination   The process of partial DNA hydrolysis by acid at purine (adenine and guanine) sites, resulting in the cleavage of large DNA fragments into smaller pieces. This process improves Southern transfer.

dermal nitrate test   An obsolete and unreliable test to determine if a person has fired a firearm. The test consists of treating paraffin casts taken of a person's hands with diphenylamine which is a reagent that reacts positively with most oxidizing agents.

derringer   The generic term applied to many variations of pocket-size pistols, either percussion or cartridge, made by manufacturers other than Henry Derringer, up to present time.

desipramine   The N-desmethyl metabolite os imipramine and is an active antidepressant agent.

detector   Apparatus of system used to detect the presence of an object, radiation of chemical compound.

detonation   An exothermic chemical reaction which propagates through reactive material at supersonic speed.

developer   A solution used to turn the latend image into a visible image on exposed films or photographic papers.

development   The movement of the mobile phase through the adsorbent layer to form a chromatogram.

deviation   As used in statistics, a departure from an expected value.

dialysis   The process of separating different size molecules in solution by means of their differential transfer across a porous membrane.

diaphragm   In optics, a device that controls the size of the aperture of a lens.

diatom   A unicellular form of alga with walls impregnated with silica.

diazepam (valium)   The second benzodiazepine derivative to have been approved for human usage and has been one of the most frequently prescribed drugs in the United States. It is administered as an antianxiety agent, muscle relaxant or anticonvulsant.

dichroism   The property of exhibiting different colors, especially two different colors, when viewed in polarized light along different axes.

die   any of various tools used to impart a specific shape to a given material.

diethylamine   Water-soluble, colorless liquid with ammonia aroma, used in rubber chemicals and pharmaceuticals and as a solvent and flotation agent.

differential extraction   A step-wise extraction procedure designed to separate intact sperm heads from lysed sperm and other cell types. The separation generally results in an enrichment of sperm DNA in one cell fraction relative to the other cell fraction. The separate fraction can be analyzed individually.

digest gel   Used in assessing the completeness of restriction enzyme digestion before proceeding to a RFLP analytical gel.

digested DNA   DNA cleaved by the action of restriction enzyme.

dimer   A compound having the same percentage composition as another, but twice the molecular weight; one formed by polymerization.

dimethylformamide   Water-white liquid; a dipolar aprotic solvent. Used as a solvent for vinyl resins and acetylene, butadiene, acid gases; catalyst in carboxylation reaction; organic synthesis.

dinitrotoluene (DNT)   An explosive used as a coating on gunpowders to retard the burning rate and to act as a moisture proofing agent.

diphenylamine   Chemical reagent used in solution with sulfuric acid and acetic acid in the dermal nitrate test. Diphenylamine is also used in smokeless powder as a stabilizer to inhibit decomposition.

diphenylcarbazide   Determination of copper and other metals.

diploid (2n)   Set of chromosomes contains two copies (2n) of each autosome and two sex chromosomes.

directionality   Relating to or indicating the direction a drop of blood traveled in space from its point of origin.

discharge   To cause a firearm to fire.

disconnector   A device to prevent a semiautomatic firearm from firing full automatic. Some pump action shotguns also have disconnectors.

disguised writing   Regardless of the result, a deliberate attempt to alter handwriting in hopes of hiding one's identity.

dispersion of birefringence The variation of birefringence with wavelength of light. When dispersion of birefringence is significant in a particular fiber, anomalous interference colors not appearing in the regular color sequence of the Michel-Levy chart may result. Strong dispersion of birefringence may also interfere with the accurate determination of retardation in highly birefringent fibers.

dispersion staining A technique for refractive index determination that employs central or annular stops placed in the objective back focal plane of a microscope. Using an annular stop with the substage iris closed, a fiber mounted in a high dispersion medium will show a colored boundary of a wavelength where the fiber and the medium match in refractive index. Using a central stop, the fiber will show colors complimentary to those seen with an annular stop.

disputed document A term suggesting that there is a argument or controversy over a document, and strictly speaking this is its true meaning. In this text, as well as through prior usage, however, "disputed document" and "questioned document" are employed interchangeably to signify a document that is under special scrutiny.

distal Indicates farther away from the center of the body.

distillation A separation process in which a liquid is converted to a vapor, and the vapor is then condensed back to a liquid. The usual purpose of distillation is separation of the compounds of a mixture. Steam distillation separates all water insoluble liquids from solids and water soluble compounds in a mixture.

distance determination The process of determining the distance from the firearm, usually the muzzle, to the target based upon pattern of gunpowder or gunshot residues deposited upon that target. Where multiple projectiles, such as shot, have been fired the spread of those projectiles is also indicative of distance.

dizygotic   Twins produced from two separate zygotes. Also called *fraternal twins*. On average, one-half of their genomes are shared.

DMAB   Paradimethylaminobenzaldehyde.

DNA (deoxyribonucleic acid)   A double chain of linked nucleotides (having deoxyribose as their sugars); the fundamental substance of which genes are composed.

DNAase (deoxyribonuclease)   An enzyme capable of cleaving DNA into small fragments.

DNA band   A DNA fragment or allele on a Southern blot autoradiogram. With reference to an identity profile, a band is a tandem repeat DNA sequence (allele) produced by cleaving a genome into fragments with a restriction enzyme having recognition sites (a) flanking the allele and (b) usually at millions of other genome locations.

DNA blot   A membrane (usually nylon) with covalently bound single-stranded DNA.

DNA contamination   The unintentional introduction of exogenous DNA into a DNA sample or PCR reaction prior to amplification.

DNA databank   Database with the collection of convicted offenders blood samples, to be used in conjunction with DNA casework to solve or link crimes where there are no known suspects.

DNA haplotype   A pattern of DNA polymorphisms.

DNA identification analysis (fingerprinting)   The characterization of one or more features of an individual's genome by developing a DNA fragment band (allele) pattern. If a sufficient number of different size bands are analyzed, the resultant bar code profile will be unique for each individual except identical twins.

DNA library (genomic of cDNA)   A collection of vectors containing fragments (a maximum of one per vector) of the total genome or cDNA of an individual.

DNA ligase   An enzyme that catalyzes nucleotide phisphodiester bond formation.

DNA polymerase   An enzyme that catalyzes the linking of deoxyribonucleotide triphosphates using complementary DNA as a template.

DNA typing   DNA typing is the term that will be used in North America as set forth by TWGDAM.

document   In its fullest meaning, any material that contains marks, symbols, or signs either visible, partially visible, or invisible that may ultimately convey a meaning or message to someone. Pencil or ink writing, typewriting, or printing on paper are the more usual forms of documents.

document examiner   An individual who scientifically studies the details and elements of documents in order to identify their source or to discover other facts concerning them. Document examiners are often referred to as handwriting identification experts, but today the work has outgrown this latter title and involves other problems than merely the examination of handwriting.

dominant gene   One which gives rise to its corresponding character, whether present in "double dose" (in the homozygote) or in "single dose" (in the heterozygote).

dot-blot   A DNA analysis system where sample DNA is directly pipetted onto a membrane, as opposed to the Southern blot procedure of enzymatic digestion, electrophoresis, and Southern transfer.

double helix   The structure of DNA first proposed by Watson and Crick, with two interlocking helices joined by hydrogen bonds between paired bases.

double-loop pattern   A whorl type of fingerprint pattern consisting of two separate loop formations and two deltas.

DPX™   A neutral medium used for mounting fibers.

DQ-alpha   A gene located in the sixth chromosome used in the dot-blot PCR method.

drawback effect   The presence of blood in the barrel of a firearm that has been drawn backward due to the effect created by discharged gasses. This is seen frequently in close-range contact gunshot injuries.

drip pattern   Blood that drips into blood resulting in round, satellite blood spatters, 0.1 to 1.0 mm in diameter, around the periphery of the central bloodstain.

driving edge, fired bullet   The driving edge of a fired bullet with a right twist is the left edge of the groove impression, or the right edge of the land impression. The driving edge of a fired bullet with left twist is the right edge of the groove impression, or the left edge of the land impression.

drug   Any natural or synthetic substance that is administered to produce specific physiological or psychological effects.

drug abuse   The non-medicinal use of a drug in a manner that is not socially acceptable.

drug dependence   The primary hazard of the abusive use of drugs is the likelihood for some individuals to develop a "need" or compulsive desire, which may occur as a result of a psychological or a physical craving.

drying oil   An organic liquid which, when applied as a thin film, readily absorbs oxygen from the air and polymerizes to form a tough elastic film. Linseed, tung, soybean and castor oils are drying oils. Under certain conditions, usually involving large surface areas and insulation, such as a pile of rags soaked with drying oils, spontaneous heating may occur.

DUI   Driving under the influence.

DWM   Deutsche Waffen und Munitions Fabriken. A German firearms manufacturer.

DWI   Driving while intoxicated.

dyes   Soluble substances that add color to textiles. Dyes are classified into groups that have similar chemical characteristics (e.g. aniline acid and azo). They are incorporated into the fiber by chemical reaction, absorption, or dispersion.

dye extraction   The removal of the dye from a fiber by incubating it in an appropriate solvent.

E

EAP   Erythrocyte acid phosphatase.

EDTA   Ethylene diamine tetracetic acid, a preservative which binds the calcium ion in blood and is found in purple stopper test tubes.

efface   To rub out, to strike or scratch out, or to erase.

ejaculate   The semen released by one ejaculation.

ejection   The act of expelling a cartridge or cartridge case from a firearm.

ejection pattern   The charting of where a particular firearm ejects fired cartridge cases.

ejection port   An opening in the receiver to allow ejection.

ejector   A portion of a firearm's mechanism which ejects or expels cartridges or cartridge cases from a firearm.

ejector marks   Toolmarks produced upon a cartridge or cartridge case on the head, generally at or near the rim, from contact with the ejector.

electric typewriter   A typewriter equipped with an electric motor that assists in operating the typebars and the carriage movements, while the typebars or type element is activated by a series of mechanical linkages.

electrolytic acid etching   Engraving the surface of a metal by electrolysis.

electrolytic photocopying   A photocopying process in which an image is projected on a sheet consisting of a paper support, a thin aluminum laminate, and a coating of a white photoconductive substance in contact with an electrolyte, and electrolysis takes place in the exposed area when a direct current is applied across the electrolyte and the aluminum underlayer.

electromagnetic radiation The energy (in the form of magnetic and electric fields) given off by a vibrating charge (such as an electron). Every physical object in the universe gives off electromagnetic radiation of one type or another. The phenomenon of sight is due to our eyes being sensitive to a certain type of electromagnetic radiation.

electron A negatively charged subatomic particle which circles the nucleus of the atom in a cloud. Most chemical reactions involve the making and breaking of bonds held together by the sharing electrons.

electron capture detector (ECD) A type of gas chromatographic detector which is sensitive to halogenated hydrocarbons and other molecules capable of easily gaining an electron. Electron capture is not generally used for hydrocarbon detection.

electronic typewriter A typewriter in which most mechanical parts have beenreplaced by electronic controls. With all such machines, mechanical linkages between the keys and the typing action are replaced by electronic circuits controlled by microprocessors, and most other actions such as escapement , fine alignment, and ribbon action, are also controlled electronically.

electropherogram Four-color image of a sequence, showing peaks that represent the bases.

electrophoresis The process of separating charged molecules, for example, negatively charged DNA fragments, in a porous medium such as agarose, by the application of an electric field. DNA separates according to size with the small fragments moving most rapidly.

electrophoretic technique   Used in the separation of common genetic marker in blood and serum.

electrophoretic mobility   A characteristic of living cells in suspension and biological commons (proteins) in solution to travel in an electric field to the positive or negative electrode, because of the charge on these substances.

element   One of 106 presently known substances that comprise all matter at and above the atomic level. A substance made up of atoms with the same atomic number; common examples are hydrogen, gold, and iron. Also known as *chemical element*.

eluant   A liquid used to extract one material from another, as in chromatography.

eluate   In serology, denotes an antibody solution made by recovery into a fluid medium of antibodies that have been taken up by red cells. Saline is usually the fluid selected and the recovery of antibodies from the red cell is effected by, for example, raising the temperature of the sensitized cells to 56°C.

elute   To remove (adsorbed material) from an adsorbent by means of a solvent. The solvent mixture which acts as the mobile phase in thin-layer chromatography.

elution   The process of removing adsorbed materials from the surface of an adsorbent such as activated charcoal. The solvent in this process is called the eluant.

emission spectroscopy   The study of the composition of substances and identification of elements by observation of the wavelength of radiation emitted by the substance as it returns to a normal state after excitation by an external source.

emulsion　A thin coating of light-sensitive material, usually silver halide in gelatin, in which the image is formed on film and photographic papers.

endonuclease　An enzyme that breaks strands of DNA at internal positions; some are involved in recombination of DNA.

endothermic reaction　A chemical reaction which absorbs heat. Also known as *endoergic*.

engraved printing　Letterheads and other matter that are printed from a metal plate containing an etched design, for example. With this type of work the ink is slightly raised above the surface of the paper.

enlargement　A print that is larger than the negative or slide; a blowup.

enzyme　A recycling protein molecule that catalyzes a specific chemical reaction. Any of a group catalytic proteins that are produced by living cells and that mediate and promote the chemical processes of life without themselves being altered or destroyed.

epithelial cells　Large cells with small round or oval nuclei, they are derived from the ureters, bladder, and urethra.

erasure (physical or chemical)　The removal of writing, typewriting, or printing from a document. It may be accomplished by either of two means: a chemical eradication in which the writing is removed or bleached by chemical agents, e.g., liquid ink eradicator; or an abrasive erasure in which the writing is effaced by rubbing with a rubber eraser or scratching out with a knife.

erythrocytes　Red blood cells. A type of blood cell that contains a nucleus in all vertebrates but man and that has hemoglobin in the cytoplasm.

escapement The spacing along the line of typewriting, that is, the basic letterspacing; also known as *pitch*.

escutcheon Area on rump of many quadrupeds which is either variously colored or has the hair specially arranged.

ESDA (electrostatic detection apparatus) Uses the principles of xerography to produce a transparency of indented impressions on documents.

Esterase D (EsD) A protein marker found in blood and other body fluid.

etamine Cotton material that is loosely woven and light-weight but has a coarse texture.

ethane A simple alkane having the formula C_2H_6. A minor component of natural gas.

ethanol C_2H_6O. Ethyl alcohol or grain alcohol as obtained from the distillation of fermented grain or starch substances.

ether Diethyl ether, ethyl ether. A highly flammable solvent which can form explosive peroxides when exposed to air. One of a class of organic compounds characterized by the structural feature of an oxygen linking two hydrocarbon groups (such as R–O–R). A colorless liquid, slightly soluble in water, used as a reagent intermediate, anesthetic, and solvent.

ethidium bromide A dye commonly used to stain DNA, rendering it visible under ultraviolet light.

ethylbenzene A component of gasoline, but also a major breakdown product or pyrolysis released when certain polymers are heated.

eukaryote A multicellular organism having true membrane-bound nuclei containing chromosomes that undergo mitosis.

eutectic   The lowest melting point of an alloy or solution of two or more substances (usually metals) that is obtainable by varying the percentage of the components. Eutectic melting sometimes occurs when molten aluminum or molten zinc comes in contact with solid steel or copper.

evaporation   Conversion of a liquid to the vapor state by the addition of latent heat.

evaporation rate   A measure of the quantity of a liquid converted to vapor in a unit of time. Among single component liquids, the rate varies directly with the surface area, the temperature and the vapor pressure, and inversely with the latent heat of vaporization of the liquid.

evolution   A stable genotype change resulting in new taxa or classification. The processes of biological and organic change in organisms by which descendants come to differ from their ancestors.

evidence sample   Sample taken from the crime scene or people or objects connected with it.

examination   The act of making a close and critical study of any material, and with questioned documents is the process necessary to discover the facts about them. Various types of examinations are undertaken, including microscopic, visual, photographic, chemical, ultraviolet, and infrared.

exclusion   A crime suspect or putative father DNA identity profile not matching that of a crime sample or offspring paternally derived alleles.

excitation fiber   A fiber used in fluorescence microscopy that transmits specific bands or wavelength of energy capable of inducing visible fluorescence in various substrates.

exemplar   A term used by some document examiners and
attorneys to characterize known material, but the author
in preparing this text has used the older, better established term, standards.

exonucleases   Cleave nucleotides one at a time from the
end of a polynucleotide chain; they maybe specific for
either the 5' or 3' end of DNA.

exothermic reaction   A chemical reaction which
evolves heat. Combustion reaction are exothermic.

expert witness   A legal term used to describe a witness
who by reason of his special technical training or experience is permitted to express an opinion regarding the
issue, or a certain aspect of the issue, which is involved
in a court action. His purpose is to interpret technical
information in his particular specialty in order to assist
the court in administering justice.

explosion   The sudden conversion of chemical energy
into kinetic energy with the release of heat, light, and
mechanical shock.

explosion limit; flammability limit   The highest or
lowest concentration of a flammable gas or vapor in air
that will explode or burn readily when ignited. This limit
is usually expressed as a volume percent of gas or vapor
in air.

explosive range, flammability range   The set of all
concentration between the upper and lower explosive
limits of a particular gas or vapor.

exponential increase   An increase at a rate defined by
raising a number to a power, e.g., 10, 10^2, 10^3.

exposure   The quantity of light allowed to act on a photographic material; a product of the intensity (controlled
by the lens opening) and the duration (controlled by the

shutter speed or enlarging time) of light striking the film or paper.

exposure meter   An instrument with a light-sensitive cell that measures the light reflected from or falling on a subject; used as an aid to selecting the exposure setting. The same as a light meter.

expressivity   The degree to which a particular genotype is expressed in the phenotype.

extension   The covalent linkage of deoxyribonucleoside triphosphates in a template-directed manner by DNA polymerase. Linkage is in a 5' to 3' direction starting from the 3' end of bound primers. PCR primers are extended one nucleotide at a time by a DNA polymerase during each PCR cycle.

extraction   A chemical procedure for removing one type of material from another. Extraction is generally carried out by immersing a solid in a liquid, or by shaking two immiscible liquids together, resulting in the transfer of a dissolved substance from one liquid to the other. Solvent extraction is one of the primary methods of sample preparation in arson debris analysis.

extractor   A mechanism for withdrawing a cartridge or cartridge case from the chamber of a firearm.

extractor mark   Toolmarks produced upon a cartridge or cartridge case from contact with the extractor. These are always found on or just ahead of the rim.

extranuclear DNA   DNA located in organelles such as mitochondria and plastids. This material is also referred to as cytoplasmic DNA and its inheritance as maternal or cytoplasmic since the organelles are transmitted only from the female via gamete cytoplasm.

F

F1 generation The first generation produced by crossing two parental (homozygous) lines.

F2 generation The second filial generation, produced by selfing or intercrossing the F1.

far-infrared Pertaining to the infrared region of the electromagnetic spectrum with wavelength range from approximately 25 to 1000_m (wavenumber range 400 to 10cm^{-1}).

Fast Salt Blue B A chemical reagent used in the identification of seminal fluid, also called Brentamine Fast blue B (O-Dianisidine Tetrazotized)

feces Anymu foul refuse matter of sediment. Animal excrement.

Federal Cartridge Company Firearms manufacturer.

feet per second The unit of measurement used to express the speed of a projectile.

fetal Pertaining to the fetus.

fiber optics A thin fiber of glass of plastic, enclosed usually in a flexible material, that will transmit light throughout its length.

fiber-tip pen (porous-tip pen) A modern writing instrument in which the marking element or point consists of a porous material through which the ink can flow. These pens are commonly known as fiber-tip or felt-tip pens or may be referred to as soft-tip pens.

FIE (Firearms Import & Export) A firearms manufacturer.

filial generation   Successive generations of progeny in a controlled series of crosses, starting with two specific parents (the P generation) and selfing or intercrossing the progeny of each new (F1, F2, ...) generation.

film   A photographic emulsion coated on a flexible, transparent, plastic base.

film speed   The sensitivity of a given film to light, indicated by a number such as ISO 200. The higher the number, the more sensitive or faster the film. ISO stands for International Standards Organization.

filter hybridization   Performed by incubating a denatured DNA preparation immobilized on a nitrocellulose filter with a solution or radioactivity labeled DNA.

fingerprint   A pattern of distinctive epidermal ridges of the bulbs of the inside of the end joints of fingers and thumbs.

fingerprint (DNA)   A DNA pattern of polymorphic restriction fragments that differ between individual genomes.

fingerprint pattern type   Formed by a series of lines, corresponding to ridges (hills) and grooves (valleys) on the skin of the fingertip. There are eight basic types of fingerprint patterns:

1. plain arch — the simplest pattern. The ridges enter on one side, rise to form a wave in the center, and exit smoothly on the opposite side.

2. tented arch — variation of the plain arch. Ridges at the center are thrust upward in a more abrupt manner similar to the appearance of a tent pole.

3. radial loop — a pattern in which one or more ridges enter on the side toward the thumb (the side on which the radius bone of the forearm lies), recurve, and then exit on the same side.

4. ulnar loop — a pattern in which one or more ridges enter on the side toward the little finger (the side on which the ulna bone of the forearm lies), recurve, and then exit toward the same side.

5. plain whorl — a pattern in which one or more ridges form a complete revolution around the center. Whorls generally have two or more deltas.

6. central pocket loop — a variation of the plain whorl pattern. Some ridges tend to form a loop pattern, which recurves and surrounds a whorl at the center.

7. double loop (twinned loop) — another type of whorl. In it two separate loop formations are present and may surround each other.

8. accidental — a relatively rare type of pattern, having three or more deltas, or having all the characteristics of two or more different pattern types (excluding the plainarch). This category is used to accommodate those patterns that do not conform to any of the patterns previously described.

fire   The light and heat manifested by the rapid oxidation of combustible materials. A flame may be manifested but is not required.

fire point   The temperature, generally a few degree above the flash point, at which burning is self-sustaining after removal of an ignition source.

fire tetrahedron   Fuel, heat, oxygen, and a chemical chain reaction.

fire triangle   Fuel, heat, and oxygen.

firearm   An assembly of a barrel and action from which a projectile(s) is propelled by products of combustion.

firearms identification   A discipline of forensic science which has as its primary concern to determine if a bullet, cartridge case or other ammunition component was fired by a particular firearm.

firing pin   That part of a firearm mechanism which strikes the primer of a cartridge to initiate ignition. Sometimes called hammer nose or striker.

firing pin impression   The indentation in the primer of a centerfire cartridge case or in the rim of a rimfire cartridge case caused when it is struck by the firing pin.

fixed ammunition   A cartridge comprised of a cartridge case, primer, propellant powder, and projectile(s).

fixed tissues   Tissues preserved with an agent such as formalin.

flame   A rapid gas phase combustion process characterized by self-propagation.

flame ionization detector (FID)   A nearly universal gas chromatographic detector. It responds to almost all organic compound. An FID does not respond to nitrogen, hydrogen, helium, oxygen, carbon monoxide, or water. This detector ionizes compounds as they reach the end of the chromatographic column by burning them in a air/hydrogen flame. As the compounds pass through the flame, the conductivity of the flame changes, generating a signal. This is the most commonly used detector in arson debris analysis.

flame propagation   Travel of a flame through a combustible gas/air or vapor/air mixture.

flammable liquid   A combustible liquid that has a flash point below 80°F according to the U.S. Coast Guard; 100°F according to the National Fire Protection Agency (NFPA). Liquids having a vapor pressure over 40 psi at 100°F are classified as flammable gases. Flammable liquids are a special group of combustible liquids.

flammable vapor   A vapor/air mixture of any concentration within the flammability range of that vapor.

flash fire   A fire that spreads with unusual speed, as one that races over flammable liquids or through combustible gases.

flash point   The temperature at which a pool of liquid will generate sufficient vapors to form an ignitable vapor/air mixture. The temperature at which a liquid will produce its lower explosive limit in air. Flash point describes one of several very specific laboratory test. Frequently, materials can be made to burn below their flash point if increased surface area or mechanical activity raises the concentration of vapor in air above the lower explosive limit.

fluorescence microscope   A variation of the compound laboratory light microscope which is arranged to admit ultraviolet, violet and sometimes blue radiations to a specimen, which then fluoresces.

fluorometric assay   The process of molecules absorbing light of one wavelength and emitting at a different (higher) wavelength.

f-number (f/#)   A number used to indicate the size and light-passing ability of the lens opening on most adjustable cameras. Common f-numbers are f/2, f/2.8, f/4, f/5.6,f/8, f/11, f/16, and f/22. The larger the f-number, the smaller the lens opening. These numbers indicate the ratio of the focal length of the lens to the effective diameter of the lens opening; f-numbers help you get the right exposure.

focal length (f)   The distance from the lens to the principal focus is a primary descriptive parameter for the lens, when considering a thin simple lens. Focal length determines image size at a given lens-to-subject distance.

focal-plane shutter   An opaque curtain containing a slit that moves directly across in front of the film in a camera and allows image-forming light to strike the film.

focal point   The point to which rays that are initially parallel to the axis of a lens, mirror, or other optical system are converged or from which they appear to diverge. Also known as *principal focus*.

focus   Adjustment of the distance setting on a lens to define the subject sharply.

foldback DNA   Consists of inverted repeats that have renatured by intrastrand reassociation of denatured DNA.

follicle   A deep, narrow sheath or a small cavity.

forcing cone   Tapered beginning of the lands at the origin of the rifling of a gun tube; the forcing cone allows the rotating band of the projectile to be gradually engaged by the rifling, thereby centering the projectile in the bore.

forend   The forward part of a one-piece stock.

forensic   Analysis of information suitable for use in a court of law.

forensic sciences   The application of scientific facts to legal problems. The field of science that is used in the judicial process. Some are derived from the physical, medical, and dental sciences, and the best-qualified workers specialize in the court-oriented aspects of each discipline.

forensic comparison microscope   Two carefully matched compound microscopes. The images produced by the two microscopes are juxtaposed in a common intermediate field plane within the ocular(s). In this manner, objects in two different fields of view can be compared directly.

forgery (freehand imitation) A legal term that involves not only a non-genuine signature or document but also an intent on the part of its maker to defraud. Any signature or holographic document written by someone other than the person himself.

formaldehyde A readily polymerizable gas. These commercial grades are called formalin. Used as embalming fluids, preservative, hardening agent, reducing agent, and durable-press treatment of textile fabrics. Highly toxic by inhalation or skin contact.

formula A combination of chemical symbols that expresses a molecule's composition. A reaction formula showing the interrelationship between reactants and products.

formula weight The gram-molecular weight of a substance.

forward spatter Blood that travels in the same direction as the source of energy or force causing the spatter. Forward spatter is often associated with gunshot wound of exit.

Founder effect Refers to the presence in a population of many individuals all with the same chromosome (or region of a chromosome) derived a single ancestor.

fountain pen A modern nib pen containing a reservoir of ink in a specially designed chamber or cartridge. After complete filling, the pen may be used to write a number of pages without refilling.

Fourier transform (FT) A mathematical operation which converts a function of one independent variable to one of a different independent variable. In FT–IR spectroscopy, the Fourier transform converts a *time* function (the interferogram) to a *frequency* function (the infrared absorption spectrum). Spectral data are collected through the use of an interferometer, which replaces the monochrometer found in the dispersive infrared spectrometer.

Fourier transform infrared (FT-IR) spectrometry
A form of infrared spectrometry in which an interferogram is obtained; this interferogram is then subjected to a Fourier transform to obtain an amplitude wavelength (or wavelength) spectrum.

fraction   One of the portions of a volatile liquid within certain boiling point ranges, such as petroleum naphtha fractions or gas-oil fractions.

fractionation   The separation of one group of compounds in a mixture from another, generally by distillation.

fragment   A piece of DNA cut by a restriction enzyme; also known as a band on an autorad.

fragment   A piece of an exploding or exploded bomb, projectile or the like.

fraudulent signature   A forged signature. It involves the writing of a name as a signature by someone other than the person himself, without his permission, often with some degree of imitation.

frame/receiver   The basic unit of a firearm which houses the firing and breech mechanism and to which the barrel and stock are assembled.

frequency   Specifically refers to the number of individuals or measurements in a subgroup of the total group under consideration. The term is often more loosely equated to proportion, that is, to define a fraction or percent. The number of times per unit time that the magnitude of an electromagnetic wave goes from maximum to minimum then back to maximum amplitude.

Frye standard   A set of standards established by the Court of Appeals of the District of Columbia in 1923 for *Frye vs. the United States*. The standards in general define when a new scientific test should be admissible as evidence in the court system.

FTIR   Fourier transform infrared spectrophotometer.

fuel oil   A heavy petroleum distillate ranging from #1 (kerosene or range oil), #2 (diesel fuel), up through #6 (heavy bunker fuels). To be identified as fuel oil, a sample must exhibit a homologous series of normal alkanes ranging from C_9 upward.

function testing   The examination of a firearm concerning its mechanical condition and operation. It is usually performed to determine if all safety features are operable and/or if the firearm is capable of firing a cartridge.

G

G   A single-letter designation of the purine base guanine

GCMS (gas chromatograph / mass spectrometer)
A quantitative and qualitative method for the separation and identification of organic materials in complex mixtures or solutions. This method has applications in the examinations of drugs, explosive residues, paints, plastics and inks and can be used to analyze material to determine if it is gunpowder.

gage   An instrument for measuring or testing. Also spelled *gauge*. The interior diameter of the barrel of a shotgun expressed by the number of spherical lead bullets fitting it that are required to make a pound.

G6PD (glucose-6-phosphate dehydrogenase)   This an enzyme, the G6PD reaction is the committed step in the pentose phosphate pathway.

gamete   A reproductive cell (egg or sperm). A specialized haploid cell that fuses with a gamete from the opposite sex or mating type to form a diploid zygote.

gas chromatograph   The instrument used in gas chromatography to detect volatile compounds present; also used to determine certain physical properties such as therm, and as a preparative technique for isolating pure components or certain fractions from complex mixtures.

gas chromatography   A separation technique involving passage of a gaseous moving phase through a column containing a fixed adsorbent phase; it is used principally as a quantitative analytical technique for volatile compounds. The separation of organic liquids of gases into discrete components or compounds seen as peaks on a chromatogram. Separation is done in a column which is enclosed in an oven held at a specific temperature, or programmed to change temperature at a reproducible rate. The column separates the compounds according to their affinity for the material inside the column (stationary phase). Columns can be packed or capillary. Packed columns employ a powdery substance which may be coated with a nonvolatile liquid phase. A capillary column is a glass or quartz tube coated with a nonvolatile liquid.

gas chromatography/mass spectrometry (GCMS)
A quantitative and qualitative method for the separation and identification of organic materials in complex mixtures or solutions. This method has applications in the examination of drugs, explosives residues, paints, plastics and inks and can be used to analyze material to determine if it is gunpowder.

gasoline A mixture of more than 20 volatile hydrocarbons in the range of C_4 to C_{12}, suitable for use in a spark ignited internal combustion engine. Regular automotive gasoline has a flash point of -40°F.

gauge A term used in the identification of a shotgun bore. The number of round lead balls of bore diameter that equal one pound. Thus 12 gauge is the diameter of a round lead ball weighing 1/12 of a pound.

gel Agarose gels used in electrophoresis.

gel electrophoresis Using a gel medium to separate charged molecules.

gene The fundamental physical and functional unit of heredity, which carries information from one generation to the next; a segment of DNA, composed of a transcribed region and a regulatory sequence that makes possible transcription.

gene cluster   A group of adjacent genes that are identical or related.

gene conversion   The alteration of one strand of a heteroduplex DNA to make it complementary with the other strand at any position(s) where there were mispaired bases.

gene dosage   Gives the number of copies of a particular gene in the genome.

gene frequency(allele frequency)   A measure of the commonness of an allele in a population; the proportion of all alleles of that gene in the population that are of this specific type.

gene locus   The specific place on a chromosome where a gene is located.

gene pair   The two copies of a particular type of gene present in a diploid cell (one in each chromosome set).

generic class   A group of fibers having similar (but not identical) chemical composition. A generic name applies to all member of a group and is not protected by trademark registration. Generic names for manufactured fibers include, for example, rayon, nylon, and polyester.

genetic variance   Phenotypic variance resulting from the presence of different genotypes in the population.

genetics   **1.** The study of genes through their variation. **2.** The study of inheritance.

genome   The entire complement of genetic material in a chromosome set.

genomic DNA   DNA sequence as it appears in the genome.

genotype The genetic make-up or hereditary blueprint of an organism..

germ cell Sex cell.

genetic markers Can be divided into two groups based on differences in biochemistry, method of detection, and history of discovery. The two groups are the polymorphic antigen system found on red cell and other cell surfaces, and the polymorphic soluble protein markers. Any allele of interest in an experiment.

glass An inorganic substance in a condition which is continuous with, and analogous to, the liquid state of that substance. An inorganic product of fusion which has cooled to a rigid condition without crystallizing. A manufactured fiber in which the fiber-forming substance is glass.

GLO I (glyoxalase I) A protein marker found in the blood and other body fluids.

glucose 6-phosphatase The enzyme that catalyses the conversion of glucose 6-phosphate to glucose plus inorganic phosphate.

glue A crude, impure, amber-colored form of commercial gelatin of unknown detailed composition produced by the hydrolysis of animal collagen; gelatinizes in aqueous solutions and dries to form a strong, adhesive layer.

grain **1.** A unit of weight (avoirdupois); 7,000 grains equal one pound. **2.** The grain unit is commonly used in American and English ammunition practice to measure the weight of components.

grain size The light-sensitive silver halides that are impregnated in the emulsion of photographic films exist as small crystals. When the film is developed are converted to pure silver granules. Microscopically, these crystals are found to vary in size with different types of films and photographic papers.

graininess The sand-like or granular appearance of a negative, print or slide resulting from the clumping of silver grains during development of the film. Graininess becomes more pronounced with faster film, increased density in the negative, and degree of enlargement.

granules The individual particles of propellant powder.

graphology The art of attempting to interpret the character of personality of an individual from his handwriting; also called grapho-analysis.

grating A reflective surface covered with evenly spaced, microscopic grooves, whose purpose is to separate the individual wavelengths from "white" light. The distance between grooves and the angle of the faces are determined by the wavelengths to be separated. The grating (except for diode arrays) is rotated at a set speed and the desired wavelength is emitted through an exit slit onto the sample or standard.

Griess test A chemical test for the detection of nitrites. It is used by the firearms examiner to develop patterns of gunpowder residues (nitrites) around bullet holes.

groove diameter The major diameter in a barrel which is the diameter of a circle circumscribed by the bottom of the grooves in a rifled barrel.

group-specific components (GC) A term applied to an antigen or hapten which possesses blood group specificity.

gunpowder Any of various powder used in firearms as a propellant charge.

gunpowder patterns **1.** The spatial distribution of gunpowder residues deposited upon a surface. **2.** The test firing of a firearm for a muzzle to target distance determination.

gunpowder residue   Unburned gunpowder, partially burned gunpowder, and smoke from completely burned gunpowder. Gunpowder residues are the largest part of gunshot residues.

guanine (G)   One of the four nucleotide that is found in DNA.

guided-hand signature   A signature that is executed while the writer's hand or arm is steadied in any way. Also known as an *assisted signature*. Under the law in most jurisdictions, such a signature authenticates a legal document provided it is shown that the writer requested the assistance. Guided signatures are most commonly written during a serious illness or on the deathbed.

gun cotton (nitrocellulose)   The principal ingredient of single-base and double-base gunpowders. Also known as *cellulose hexanitrate*.

gunshot residue   The total residues resulting from the discharge of a firearm. It includes both gunpowder and primer residues, plus metallic residues from projectiles, fouling, ect.

GYPA   Glyophorin A.

gyroscpic stability   The ability of a fired bullet to remain stable in flight due to its spin.

H

habit   Any repeated element or detail that may serve to individualize writing.

Hae III restriction enzyme   Derived from bacteria, it catalyzes the cleavage of DNA at specific points.

hair   An appendage of the skin that grows out of an organ known as the hair follicle. A thread-like outgrowth of the epidermis of animals, especially a keratinized structure in mammalian skin.

half-cock   The position of the hammer of a firearm when about half retracted and held by the sear so that it cannot be operated by a normal pull of the trigger.

hammer   A component part of the firing mechanism which gives impulse to the firing pin or primer.

handguard   A wooden, plastic, or metal type of forend/forearm that generally encircles the forward portion of the barrel to protect the hand from heat when firing.

handgun   A firearm designed to be held and fired with one hand.

handlettering (handprinting)   Any disconnected style of writing in which each letter is written separately.

hangfire   Any delay in firing of an abnormal duration; implies that firing does eventually occur.

haploid (n)   The nuclear state in which only one member of each homologous chromosome pair is present, for example, human gametes (egg or sperm).

haplotype   The particular combination of alleles in a defined region of some chromosome, in effect the genotype in miniature. Originally used to describe combinations of major histocompatability complex (MHC) alleles, it now may be used to describe particular combination of restriction fragment length polymorphism (RFLPs).

hapten   A small molecule that acts as an antigen when conjugated to a protein.

haptoglobin (Hp)   A blood serum protein which binds hemoglobin.

Hardy-Weinberg equilibrium   In a large random intrabreeding population, not subjected to excessive selection or mutation, the gene and genotype frequencies will remain constant over time. The sum $p^2 + 2pq + q^2$ applies at equilibrium for a single allele pair where p is the frequency of allele A, q the frequency of a, p^2 the frequency of genotype AA, q^2 the frequency of aa, and $2pq$ the frequency of Aa.

Harrington & Richardson   A firearms manufacturer.

headspace concentration   A technique for concentration all or most of the flammable or combustible liquid vapors in a sample onto a tube of charcoal, a wire coated with charcoal, a charcoal coated polymer, or some other adsorbing material which will later be desorbed in order to analyze the concentrated vapor. This is a primary form of sample preparation in arson debris analysis. This is also known as adsorption/elution, vapor concentration, or total headspace.

headstamp   Numerals, letters, and symbols (or combinations thereof) stamped into the head of a cartridge case or shotshell to identify the manufacture, caliber, gauge, or give additional information.

headspace　The distance from the face of the closed breech of a firearm to the surface in the chamber on which the cartridge case bears.

headspace gage　An instrument for measuring the distance from the breech face of a firearm to that portion of the chamber against which the cartridge bears.

heat　A mode of energy associated with and proportional to molecular motion that may be transferred from one body to another by conduction, convection or radiation.

heel　**1.** The part of a rifle or shotgun stock at the top of the butt end. **2.** The rear portion of a bullet or its base.

helix　Any structure with a spiral shape. The Watson and Crick model of DNA is in the form of a double helix.

helixometer　**1.** An instrument for inspecting the interior of a gun barrel and for measuring the rate of twist of the rifled bore of a firearm. **2.** The geometry of a rifled barrel described as a helix. Developed in 1925, in New York by John H. Fisher of the "Bureau of Forensic Ballistics."

hemoglobin (Hb)　The iron-containing, oxygen-carrying molecule, pigment of red blood cells compound of two α-chain, two β-chains, and heme group.

heptane　An alkane having the formula C_7H_{16}, flash point of 25°F and explosive limit of 1.2% to 6.7%.

heredity　The biological similarity of offspring and parents.

heterochromatin　Nontranscribed, late replicating, repetitious chromosomal DNA.

heteroduplex (hybrid) DNA　Generated by base pairing between complementary single strands derived from the different parental duplex molecules; it occurs during genetic recombination.

heterogametic sex   The sex that produces gametes each with either an X or Y chromosome. In mammals, the Y-bearing sperm are male determinant and the X female.

heterologous   Refers to segments of DNA derived from different sources.

heterozygote   An individual with different alleles at some particular locus.

heterozygous   The presence of different alleles at corresponding homologous chromosome loci.

hexane   An alkane having the formula C_6H_{14}. Hexane has a flash point of -9°F and an explosive limit of 1.2% to 7.5%.

highly repetitive DNA   The first component to reassociate and is equated with satellite DNA.

high-velocity impact spatter   A bloodstain pattern caused by a high-velocity force characterized by a mistlike dispersion which, owing to the low density of the blood particles, has traveled only a short distance in flight. A high-velocity impact is considered to be approximately 100 feet per second or greater such as produced by gunshot and high-speed machinery. Individual stains within the mistlike dispersion are usually 0.1 mm or smaller in diameter but may be seen in association with larger bloodstains.

hinged frame   Any of a large array of pistols, revolvers, shotguns, and rifles whose frames are hinged to facilitate loading and ejection. Generally, the barrel(s) pivot downward.

HLA (human leukocyte antigen)   Antigens located on the surface of most cells, excluding red blood cells and sperm. These antigens are closely associated with transplant rejection. They are frequently used in individual identification, particularly in paternity determination.

HLA-DQ alpha locus   A gene located in the sixth chromosome used in PCR. A member of the Class II group of HLA, which are found on the surface of some lymphoctyes and macrophages.

holographic document   Any document completely written and signed by one person; also known as a holograph. In a number of jurisdictions a holographic will can be probated without anyone having witnessed its execution.

holster stock   A holster, usually made of wood, which attaches to the rear of the pistol grip of certain handguns and serves as a shoulder stock.

homogametic sex   The sex that produces gametes with only one type of sex chromosome. In mammals, each egg carries one X chromosome. Sperm carry an X or a Y chromosome.

homologous   Refers to the chromosome pairs found in diploid organisms. The human has 22 homologous pairs of autosomes (non-sex chromosomes) plus two sex chromosomes per nucleus. The members of each pair have an identical sequence of genes; however, the alleles at corresponding loci may be identical (homozygous) or different (heterozygous).

homologous series   A series of similar organic compounds, differing only in that the next higher member of the series has an additional CH_2 group (one carbon atom and two hydrogen atoms) in its molecular structure. Fuel oils are characterized by the presence of identifiable homologous series of normal alkanes.

homozygote   An individual with the same allele at corresponding loci on the homologous chromosomes.

homozygous   The presence of identical alleles at corresponding homologous chromosome loci.

horizontal malalignment   An alignment defect in which the character prints to the right or left of its proper position.

human chorionic gonadotropin (HCG)   A gonadotropic and leuteotropic hormone secreted by the chorionic vesicle.

hybridization   The pairing of complementary strands of DNA, or RNA and DNA, derived from different sources.

hydrocarbon   An organic compound containing only carbon and hydrogen.

hydrochloric acid   Pertaining to or designating a colorless, corrosive, fuming acid, HCl, exceedingly soluble in water. A chemical reagent used in the sodium rhodizonate test for lead and other primer residues.

hydrogen   The simplest element. Atomic number 1. Hydrogen gas has a specific gravity of 0.694 (air = 1), so it is much lighter than air. Hydrogen is highly flammable, forming water upon combustion. Explosive limit are 4% to 75%.

hydrogen bond   A relatively weak bond between a hydrogen (H) atom, covalently bound to a nitrogen (N) or oxygen (O) atom, and another atom. These bonds bind complimentary DNA strands. They can be broken by increasing temperature.

hydrolytic reaction   one in which a covalent bond is broken with the incorporation of a water molecule.

hydrophilic   Groups interact with water, so that hydrophilic regions of protein or the faces of a lipid bilayer reside in an aqueous environment. Having a strong affinity for binding or absorbing water, which results in swelling and formation of reversible gels.

hydrophobic Groups repels water, so that they interact with one another to generate a nonaqueous environment. Antagonistic to water; incapable of dissolving in water.

hygroscopic Substances which absorb or attract moisture from the air.

hyperchromicity The increase in optical density that occurs when DNA is denatured.

hypervariable region A segment of a chromosome characterized by considerable variation in the number of tandem repeats at one or more loci.

hypothesis A reasonable suggestion that remains to be proven. A proposition which is thought to be true because its consequences are found to be true.

I

identifiable striae   Striations in the evidence mark which can be identified with reproduced striations in the test marks.

IEF   Isoelectric focusing is one of the simplest techniques for separation and characterization of proteins.

ignition   The means by which burning is started.

ignition temperature   The minimum temperature to which a fuel must be heated in order to initiate or cause self-sustained combustion independent of another heat source.

imbricate   Having overlapping edges, such as scales or the petals of a flower.

IMI   Israel Military Industries. A firearms manufacturer.

immiscible   Describes substances of the same phase or state of matter (usually liquid) that cannot be uniformly mixed or blended.

immunoassay   A fluorescent antibody technique, used for detection of antigens and antibodies in blood and serum.

immunochemistry   That branch of chemistry concerned with the various defense mechanisms of the animal organism against infective agents, particularly the response between the body and foreign macromolecules (antigens), and the interaction between the products of the response (antibodies) and the agents that have elicited them. This involves study of the many proteins involved in these responses.

immunodiffusion   It involves the use of agar plates with wells for both antibodies and antigens. The two reactants diffuse into the gel where immunoprecipitates will form at the point of equivalence for each antigen-antibody pair.

immunoelectrophoresis   Consists of a combination of electrophoresis and immunodiffusion in a gel. It is based on the fact that in a gel medium, the movement of molecules in an electric field is similar to that in a liquid medium, with the advantage that free diffusion is lessened after electrophoresis. This method is used only for qualitative comparison of the protein in different samples.

immunogenetics   Molecular genetics of the immune system.

impact/penetration damage   The bullet or projectile strike on a target.

impact site   The point on a bloody object or body which receives a blow. Often, impact site is used interchangeably with point of origin. Impact site may also refer to an area on the surface of a target which is struck by blood in motion.

impact velocity   The velocity of a projectile or missile at the instant of impact. Also known as *striking velocity*.

Impramine   The prototype of the tricyclic antidepressant drugs.

impurity   The presence of one substance in another in such low concentration that it cannot be measured quantitatively by ordinary analytical methods.

inbreeding   Reproduction between related individuals.

incandescence   The emission of visible radiation by a hot body.

incendiaries Substances or mixtures of substances consisting of a fuel and an oxidizer used to initiate a fire.

incendiary fire Fire intentionally set by human hands often involving the use of an accelerant to spread and increase the rate and intensity of burning.

incidental accelerants Flammable or combustible liquids which are usual and incidental to an area where they are detected. Gasoline is incidental to an area where gasoline-powered appliances are kept. Kerosene is incidental to an area where a kerosene heater is kept. Flammable liquids may also comprise a part of a product such as insecticide, furniture polish, or paint. Additionally, certain asphalt-containing building materials may yield detectable quantities of fuel oil components.

inclusion A crime suspect or putative father DNA identity profile matching that of a crime sample or offspring paternally derived alleles.

incriminating value (IV) The ratio of the probability (x) of a match for the characteristic measured if the suspect and crime specimens are from the same source to the probability (y) if they are from different sources. $IV = x \div y$.

individual characteristics A characteristics that is highly personal or peculiar and is unlikely to occur in other instances. Traits that define and identify an item as unique; exclusive to all other items.

individual A unique item; identified as itself to the exclusion of all other items.

infrared The region of the electromagnetic spectrum including wave lengths from 0.78 to 1000_m (wavenumber range 20,000 to 4,000 cm^{-1}).

infrared absorption The taking up of energy from infrared radiation by a medium through which the radiation is passing.

infrared examination The examination of documents employing invisible radiation beyond the red portion of the visible spectrum. Infrared radiation can be recorded on specially sensitized photographic emulsions or it can be converted by means of an electronic viewing device into visible light for an on-the-scene study of the evidence.

infrared luminescence A phenomenon encountered with some dyes used in inks and colored pencils that, when illuminated with a narrow band of light in the blue-green portion of the spectrum, give off a luminescence that can be detected in the far-red or near-infrared range. The technique is useful in distinguishing between certain inks and colored pencils, and in detecting or deciphering erasures.

infrared spectrometer Device used to identify and measure the concentration of heteronatomic compound in gases, in many nonaqueous liquids and in some solids.

infrared spectrophotometry (IR) An analytical technique which utilizes an instrument which passes infrared radiation through a sample or which bounces infrared radiation off the surface of a sample. A very sensitive heat detecting device measures the amount of infrared radiation absorbed as the wavelength of the radiation reaching the detector is changed. IR can give useful information about the type of compounds present in a sample, but it is not capable of precisely identifying a complex mixture. Infrared is very useful in identifying single solvent accelerants. Operates in the IR wavelength range. IR is employed by forensic scientists in the analysis of drugs, plastics, fibers, paint, and similar substances.

infrared spectroscopy   The study of the properties of material systems by means of their interaction with infrared radiation; ordinarily the radiation is dispersed into a spectrum after passing through the material.

inhibitor   A chemical used to slow or stop a disliked reaction. In manufacturing powder propellants, it is used to decrease the burning rate. Any substance or object that retards a chemical reaction; a major or modifier gene that interferes with a reaction.

inhibition   The prevention of the normal reaction between an antigen and its corresponding antibody, usually because an antigen of the same specificity, but from another source, is present in the system—hence, to inhibit.

injection port   The area on a gas chromatograph or a high-performance liquid chromatography where the sample is introduced into the instrument and onto the column.Ink eradicator   A chemical solution capable of bleaching ink.

inorganic chemistry   The study of chemical reactions and properties of all the elements and their compounds, with the exception of hydrocarbons, and usually including carbides, oxides of carbon, metallic carbonates, carbon-sulfur compounds, and carbon-nitrogen compounds.

inorganic fiber   A class of fibers of natural mineral origin (e.g., chrysotile asbestos) and man-made mineral origin (e.g., fiberglass).

inorganic pigment   A natural or synthetic metal oxide, sulfide, or other salt used as a coloring agent for paints, plastics, and inks.

insertion The addition of writing and other material within a document such as between line or paragraphs, or the addition of whole pages to a document.

interference colors Colors produced by the interference of two out-or-phase rays of white light when a birefringence material is observed at a nonextinction position between crossed polars. The retardation at a particular point in a birefringent fiber may be determined by comparing the observed interference color to Michel-Levy chart.

interlineation The act of inserting writing or typewriting between two lines of writing.

internal reflection spectroscopy (IRS) The technique or recording optical spectra by placing a sample material in contact with a transparent medium of greater refractive index and measuring the reflectance (single or multiple) from the interface, generally at angles of incidence greater than the critical angle.

intumescent char In plastics, the swelling and charring which results in a higher ignition point. Used in the preparation of flame retardant materials. *In vitro* means "in glass" and refers to a biological process carried out in the laboratory separate from an organism.

in vivo Refers to a biological process within a living organism.

ion An atom, molecule or radical that has lost or gained one or more electrons, thus acquiring an electric charge. Positively charged ions are cations; negatively charged ions are anions.

iron-gallotannate ink This ink is found in fountain pens, was used as early as the eighth century and with substantial improvement is still in use today. Iron salts are combined with gallotannic acid in an aqueous solution. This solution when applied to paper is first color-less but darkens quickly when oxidized by air.

ISFH   International Society for Forensic Haemogenetics.

isomer   One of two or more forms of a chemical compound which have the same number and type of each atoms, but a different arrangement of atoms.

isoparaffins   A mixture of branched alkanes usually available as a narrow "out" of a distillation. Exxon manufactures a group of products known as "isopars" ranging from isopar A through isopar J. These solvent mixtures have a variety of uses. Gulf Oil manufactures a similar series of solvents, the most commonly available of which is Gulf Lite Charcoal Starter Fluid which is roughly equivalent to Exxon's isopar G.

isothermal   A type of gas chromatographic analysis wherein the column is maintained at a uniform temperature throughout the analysis.

isotope   One of two or more forms or species of an element that have the same atomic number, i.e., the same position in the Periodic Table, but different atomic masses.

isotropic   Singly refracting in polarised light. An object which is identical in all directions; invariant with respect to direction.

isozyme   One of several forms of a specific enzyme. Different isozymes may be most efficient under different environmental conditions such as temperature and pH. Any of the electrophorectically distinct forms of an enzyme, representing different polymeric states but having the same function. Also known as *isoenzyme*.

Ithaca Gun Company   A firearms manufacturer.

Iver Johnson   A firearms manufacturer.

IVI–Valcartier Industries   A firearms manufacturer.

J

jacket   Cylinder of steel covering and strengthening the breech end of a gun; the envelope enclosing the lead core.

justification   In type composition, the adjustment of spacing in each line of type so that all lines are filled out to the same desired length.

K

karyotype   An individual's set of chromosomes. Chromosomes arranged in order of length and according to position of centromere; also the abbreviated formula for the chromosome constitution, such as 47, XX + 21 for human trisomy–21.

kb (kilobase)   An abbreviation for 1000 base pairs of DNA

Kernechtrot solution   A reddish stain which is used in conjunction with picroindigocarmine solution in the identification of human sperm. The solution will turn the head of the sperm a reddish-pink color.

kerosene (#1 fuel oil)   Flash point generally between 100 and 150° F. Explosive limits of 0.7% to 5.0%. Kerosene consists mostly of C_9 through C_{17} hydrocarbons. In order to be identified as kerosene, a sample extract must exhibit a homologous series five consecutive normal alkanes between C_9 and C_{17}. Kerosene is the most common "incidental" accelerant, as it is used in numerous household products ranging from charcoal lighter fluid to lamp oil to paint thinner to insecticide carriers. It is used as jet fuel. K-1 kerosene has a low sulfur content required for use in portable space heaters.

ketamine   Primarily used as an animal anesthetic.

ketone   A type of organic compound having a carbonyl functional group ($C = O$) attached to two alkyl groups. Acetone is the simplest example of a ketone.

kilo   A prefix representing 10^3 or 1000. Abbreviated k.

kinetics   A dynamic process involving motion.

knit fabric   A structure produced by interloping one or more ends of yarn or comparable material.

known (samples)   A subset of a larger population or sample originating from a verifiable source, collected as representative of that larger grouping.

known standards   A collection and cataloging of test fired bullets and cartridge cases from known firearms. Also known as *fired standards*.

knurls; knurling   Regularly spaced ridges or rectangles used on a metal surface to assist in the prevention of slippage, usually on a knob.

L

land   The raised portion between the grooves in a rifled bore.

land and groves impressions (right and left turns)
The negative impressions on the surface of a bullet caused by the rifling in the barrel from which it was fired.

lane of gel   The path in the gel within which DNA fragments migrate.

laser   A device that uses the maser principle of amplification of electromagnetic waves by stimulated emission of radiation and operates in the optical or infrared regions.

latent image   The invisible image left by the action of light on photographic film or paper. The light changes the photosensitive salts to varying degrees depending on the amount of light striking them. When processed, this latent image will become a visible image either in reversed tones (as in a negative) or in positive tones (as in a color slide).

latent print   Is generally used to describe any type of print found at the scene of a crime or on evidence associated with a crime. Latent prints are normally not visible. Some means of development is generally required for their visualization.

lattes crust method   This method relies upon the presence of the agglutinins in a bloodstain and is applicable only to the ABO system. Adding indicator cells to the blood crust or bloodstain and testing for agglutination, is a convenient way to detect the presence of agglutinin.

LDRL   Low-density lipoprotein receptor.

lead glass   Glass into which lead oxide is incorporated to give high refractive index, optical dispersion, and surface brilliance; used in optical glass.

leading   The accumulation of lead in the bore of a firearm from the passage of lead shot or bullets. Also called *metal fouling*.

left-handed or wrong-handed writing   Any writing executed with the opposite hand from that normally used. Sometimes refered to as writing "with the awkward hand." It is an attempt to disguise. Thus, the writing of a right-handed person written with his left hand accounts for the common terminology for this class of disguise as "left-handed writing."

lens   One or more pieces of optical glass or similar material designed to collect and focus rays of light to form a sharp image on the film, paper or projection screen.

lens speed   The largest lens opening (smallest f-number) at which a lens can be set. A fast lens transmits more light and has a larger opening than a slow lens. Is a measure of the light-gathering power of a lens.

leucomalachite green (leuco)   A catalytic test which is used for the detection of blood and blood stains. The test depends upon an oxidation reaction in which an oxidant, such as hydrogen peroxide, oxidizes a colorless material such as phenolphthalein to a colored one.

lever action   A design wherein the breech mechanism is cycled by an external lever generally below the receiver.

lidocaine   A crystalline compound, used as a local anesthetic.

Liebmann effect   The effect whereby it is more difficult to visually distinguish contrasting forms when they have the same luminance and different chromaticities than when they have different and the same chromaticity.

lift-off ribbon   A modern typewriting ribbon whose ink can be completely removed with a special adhesive tape to leave an apparent blank area; also sold as a correctable ribbon.

ligand   A molecule, ion, or atom that is attached to the central atom of a coordination compound, a chelate, or other complex.

ligase   An enzyme that joins the ends of two strands of nucleic acid.

ligation   The joining of two or more DNA molecules by covalent bonds.

light   **1.** The natural condition or medium permitting vision. **2.** Any one of a number of known forms of radiant energy which travels with a wave motion.

light microscope   A microscope that employs light in the visible or near-visible portion of the electromagnetic spectrum.

lighting   The illumination falling on a subject, particularly the direction or arrangement of the illumination.

lignin   The majority noncarbohydrate portion of wood. It is an amorphous polymeric substance that cements cellulosic fibers together. The principal constituents of woody cell walls.

line quality   A term characterizing the visible record in the written stroke of the basic movements and manner of holding the writing instrument. It is derived from a combination of factors including writing skill, speed, rhythm, freedom of movement, shading, and pen position.

likelihood   A statistical measure of the correctness of a hypothesis given certain observations.

likelihood ratio   The probability of a random drawing of a specified sample from a population, assuming a given hypothesis about the parameters of the population, divided by the probability of a random drawing of the same sample, assuming that the parameters of the population are such that this probability is maximized.

linkage   A measure of association between loci. Loci on different chromosomes are nonlinked. Those close together on the same chromosome are closely linked and are usually inherited together.

linkage disequilibrium   The phenomenon of a specific allele of one locus being associated or linked to a specific allele or marker of another locus, on the same chromosome, with a greater frequency than expected by chance.

linkage group   The genes located on a single chromosome.

litigation   To contest the law.

locus (plural, loci)   The site on a chromosome where a gene or a defined sequence is located. The position on a chromosome occupied by a gene.

longitudinal   Pertaining to the lengthwise dimension.

low-velocity impact spatter   Bloodstains produced on a surface when the blood source has been subjected to a low-velocity force approximately 5 feet per second or less.

LSD (lysergic acid diethylamide)   A drug which can induce a psychotic like state. A psychotomimetic drug synthesized from compounds derived from ergot.

Luger   A German automatic pistol widely used in Europe as a military sidearm: manufactured in various calibers, most commonly 7.65 mm. and 9 mm.

lumen   The cavity or central canal present in many natural fibers (e.g. cotton, flax, ramie, jute, hemp). Its presence and structure are often a useful aid in identification.

lumigraph   A sheet of X-ray film with the results of quantified DNA, which is measured in ng/ul.

Lumi-Phos Plus®   A detection reagent, when added to a hybridized membrane which triggers a light generating reaction.

Luminol test   Method of choice for the detection of occult (not noticeable to the eye) blood at a crime scene that was cleaned up or escaped detection for extended periods of time.

luster   The gloss of shine possessed by a fiber, resulting from its reflection of light. The luster of manufactured fibers is often modified by use of a delustering pigment.

lymphocyte   A general class of white blood cells that are important components of the immune system of vertebrate animals.

lyocel   A manufactured fiber composed of precipitated cellulose and produced by a solvent extrusion process where no chemical intermediates are formed.

lysis agent   A chemical used to open the cell membrane and cell nucleus and free the DNA

lysis   The breakdown of cells.

M

machine defect　Any defect in typewriting resulting from the malfunctioning of the machine rather than the typebar or type element. Normally, these defects include improper escapement spacing (that is, each letter underspaces or overspaces a fraction of the basic unit) and defects in printing brought about by improper alignment of the typing unit and the roller. In other words, machine defects tend to affect all the characters on the machine rather than any particular character.

magazine clip　A container for cartridges which has a spring and follower to feed the cartridges into the chamber of a firearm.

magnesium (Mg)　A silvery metal used in some metal incendiaries. The dust is highly explosive. Ignition point of 650°F.

major criminal prints　A recording of all of the friction ridges skin that covers the hands. Major criminal prints include fingers, palm, tips of the fingers, and middle joints of the fingers both sides.

Mannlicher-type bolt　A bolt-action rifle which was designed for the receiver bridge has a gap at the top to allow passage of the bolt handle.

manual typewriter　A machine whose operation depends solely upon the mechanical action set in motion by striking a letter or character key. During the first 50 or more years in typewriter history, all machines were manually operated.

manufactured fiber   A class name of various families of fibers produced from fiber-forming substances which may be synthesized polymers, modified or transformed natural polymers and glass.

manuscript writing   A disconnected form of script or semiscript writing. This type of writing is taught young children in elementary schools as the first step in learning to write.

margin justification (left or right)   *See* Justification.

marker (DNA)   A fragment of known size used to calibrate an electrophoretic gel.

marker (genetic)   Is any allele of interest in an experiment.

Marlin Firearms   A firearms manufacturer.

mass spectrometer   A mass spectroscope in which a slit moves across the paths of particles with various masses, and an electrical detector behind it records the intensity distribution of masses.

mass spectrometry   An analytical technique for identification of chemical structures, determination of mixtures, and quantitative elemental analysis, based on application of the mass spectrometer. A method of chemical analysis which vaporizes, then ionizes the substance to be analyzed, and then accelerates the ions through a magnetic field to separate the ions by molecular weight. Mass spectrometry can result in the exact identification of an unknown compound, and is a very powerful analytical technique, especially when combined with chromatography.

maternal   Pertaining to, or related to a mother.

maternal inheritance   Describes the preferential survival in the progeny of genetic markers provided by one parent. A type of uniparental inheritance in which all progeny have the genotype and phenotype of the parent acting as the female.

matrix Consists of at least 5 fluorescently labeled DNA fragments for each dye, run and analyzed in separate lane.

matrix-substrate The material from which a substance of interest is removed for analysis.

mean (arithmetic) A statistical measure of central tendency equating to an arithmetic average of a group of values.

median A statistical measure of central tendency equating to the mid value in a ranked series.

medium-velocity impact spatter Bloodstains produced on a surface when the blood source has been subjected to a medium-velocity force between approximately 5 and 25 feet per second.

medulla Marrow of bones; central part of an organ or tissue; pith or central portion of stem. The central portion of a hair composed of a series of discrete cells or an amorphous spongy mass. A cellular column running through the center of the cortex. It may be air-filled, and if so, will appear opaque or black using transmitted light or white using reflected light. In animal hair, several types have been defined: uni- or multi-serial ladder, cellular or vacuolated, and lattice.

mega- Prefix meaning 10^6 units (symbol M). 1 megagram equals 1,000,000 grams.

meiosis The process whereby a sex cell nucleus, after chromosomal replication, divides twice to form four nuclei each with one-half the original chromosome number.

melanin Black or dark-brown pigment.

melt The process of disrupting the hydrogen bonds linking complementary DNA strands.

melting The denaturation point in referring to DNA.

melting point The melting point or freezing point of a pure substance is the temperature at which its crystals are in equilibrium with the liquid phase at atmosphere pressure.

melting temperature (Tm) The midpoint of the temperature range over which DNA is denatured.

membranes Consists of an asymmetrical lipid bilayer that has lateral fluidity and contains proteins. The coating of a biological cell, in and through which the osmotic mechanism of nutrient supply operates.

Mendel's laws **1.** Segregation: during meiosis only one member of each homologous chromosome pair is transferred to a specific gamete. **2.** Independent assortment:during meiosis the members of the different homologous chromosome pairs assort independently when transferred to a specific gamete, for example: AA′ and BB′ homologous chromosome pairs could give rise to AB, AB′, A′B or A′B′ possible gametes.

meperidine hydrochloride A fine, white, odorless, crystalline powder; very soluble in water, soluble in alcohol, and its uses in medicine as a narcotic.

mercerized cotton Cotton which has been strengthened by passing through a 25 to 30% solution of sodium hydroxide under tension, and then washed with water while under tension. This causes the fibers to shrink, increases their strength an attraction for colors, as well as imparting luster.

mercuric iodide Red, tetragonal crystals, turns yellow when heated to 150°C. Used in medicine and analytical reagents (Nessler's reagent and Mayer's reagent).

mercury bath A process using mercury for the removal of lead residue from a barrel.

metabolism The chemical change, constructive and destructive, occurring in living organisms. The chemical transformations occurring in an organism from the time a nutrient substance enters it until it has been utilized and the waste products eliminated.

metabolite An intermediate material produced and used in the processes of a living cell or organism. Metabolites are used for replacement and growth in living tissue, and are also broken down to be a source of energy in the body.

meta-ethyltoluene (m-ethyltoluene) A compound of gasoline.

metallic paint Paint used for covering metal surfaces; the pigment is commonly iron oxide.

metallic pigment Thin, opaque aluminum or copper alloy flakes that are incorporated into plastic masses to produce metallike effects.

metameric pair Two colors that appear the same under one illumination, but different under color illumination.

meter The basic unit of length of the metric system, abbreviated m.

methadone hydrochloride A synthetic narcotic. Used medicinally as a sedative and also useful in treating heroin addiction.

methamphetamine Colorless, volatile liquid; characteristic strong odor and slightly burning taste. Highly toxic. Flammable, dangerous fire risk. Basis of a group of hallucinogenic, habit-forming drugs which affects the CNS.

methane The simplest hydrocarbon and the first member of the paraffin (alkane) series, having a formula CH_4.

Methane is the major constituent of natural gas. Methane has a heating value of 1000 BTU/cubic foot. Its explosive limits are 5% to 15%.

methanol   Methyl alcohol. Wood alcohol. The simplest alcohol. Methanol is water soluble and has a flash point of 54°F and explosive limits of 6% to 36.5%.

methyl silicone   A nonvolatile oily liquid used in gas chromatography to separate nonpolar compounds. Methyl silicone columns typically separate compounds according to their boiling point.

methylstyrene   A common polymer pyrolysis product.

Michel-Levy chart   A chart relating thickness, birefringence, and retardation so that any one of these variables can be determined for an anisotropic fiber when the other two are known.

micro-   A prefix representing 10^6, or one-millionth.

microfuge   A high-speed (usually 10,000 + rpm) centrifuge for centrifugation of small (usually < 2 ml) specimens.

micrometer   An instrument for measuring very small distances or dimensions. A caliper or gage arranged to allow of minute measurements. Abbreviated (m. Also known as *micron* (μm).

microphotograph   Copies of documents at a greatly reduced scale on small film sizes. They are used in certain commercial record systems.

microscopical   Concerning a microscope or the use of a microscope.

microscopist   An individual who uses a microscope to examine minute particles, hairs, fibers and objects unable to be seen by the naked eye.

**microscopic examination (microscopic compari-
son)**   Any study or examination made with the microscope in order to discover minute physical details.

microscopy   The analytical approach in which a microscope playf useful information from a variety of samples.

microspectrophotometer   A split-beam or double-beam
spectrophotometer including a microscope for the local-
ization of the object under study, and capable of carrying
out spectral analyses within the dimensions of a single
cell.

microspectroscope   An instrument for analyzing the
spectra of microscopic objects, such as living cells, in
which light passing through the sample is focused by a
compound microscope system. This light and the light
which has passed through a reference sample are dispersed by a prism spectroscope, so that the spectra of
both can be viewed simultaneously.

microtome   An instrument for making very thin sections
for microscopic observations.

mid-infrared   Pertaining to the infrared region of the
electromagnetic spectrum with wavelength range from
approximately 2.5 to 25_m (wavelength range 4000 to
400 cm^{-1}).

mineral spirits   A medium petroleum distillate ranging
from C_8 to C_{12}. The flash point of mineral spirits is
generally around 100°F. Mineral spirits, sometimes
known as mineral turps, is commonly used as a solvent
in insecticides and certain other household products.
Many charcoal lighter fluids are composed almost
entirely of mineral spirits.

minisatellites   Regions of tandem repeats sequence DNA scattered throughout animal (and probably plant) genomes.

minutiae   The characteristics which make each fingerprint capable of being differentiated from any other print by a different area of friction skin. Comparison of latent prints with known prints begins with the overall pattern. The ridge detail of fingerprints, including the ends of the ridges, their separations, and their relationships to one another, constitute the bases for fingerprint comparison.

misfire   The failure of the igniting primer to ignite the powder.

mitochondrion   A DNA containing cytoplasmic organelle of eukaryotes. Mitochondria are referred to as the powerhouses of the cell because of the site for ATP production. The DNA in the mitochondria has a maternal inheritance.

mitosis   The cell division which produces daughter cells with the same number of chromosomes as the original cells. All cell division, with the exception of that which produces mature sex cells, is mitotic.

mixture   A heterogeneous blend of elements or compound which may or may not be uniformly dispersed. All solutions are uniformly dispersed mixtures.

mobile phase   The moving liquid phase used for development. In gas chromatography, the mobile phase is the inert carrier gas that moves the volatile analytes through the length of the column.

modacrylic fiber   Generic name for a manufactured fiber in which the fiber-forming substance is any long chain synthetic polymer composed of less than 85% but at least 35% by weight of acrylonitrile units. Characterized by moderate tenacity, low water absorption, and resistance to combustion. Self-extinguishing.

model signature   A genuine signature that has been used to prepare an imitated or traced forgery.

modification ratio   A geometrical parameter used in the characterization of noncircular fiber cross-sections. The modification ratio is the ratio in size between the outside diameter of the fiber and the diameter of the core. It may also be called "aspect ratio."

molal   A concentration in which the amount of solute is stated in moles and the amount of solvent in kilograms.

molar   A concentration in which one molecular weight in grams (one mole) of a substance is dissolved in one liter of solution. Molarity is indicated by an italic capital M. Molar quantities are proportional to the molecular weight of the substance.

molecular biology   A subdivision of biology that approaches the subject of life at the level of molecular size. This applies to phenomena occurring within the cell nucleus, where the chromosomes and genes are located.

molecular genetics   The study of the molecular processes underlying gene structure and function.

molecular weight (MW)   The sum of the atomic weights of all of the atoms within a molecule. Generally, molecules of the same type have higher boiling points if the molecular weight is higher.

molecule   The smallest particle into which a substance can be divided without changing its chemical properties. A molecule of an element consists of one atom, or two or more atoms that are similar. A molecule of a compound consists of two or more different atoms.

Mongoloid   Of or pertaining to the so-called yellow race, with skin color varying from light yellow to light brown, head hair straight to wavy, sparse body hair, broad nose, high cheek bones, and dark eyes with marked epicanthic folds.

monochromatic light   Radiation consisting of a single wavelength.

Monochrome[307] **(USA)**   Trademark for a series of mordant dyestuffs. Used for the dyeing of wool. Characterized by good fastness properties.

monomer   The simplest unit of a polymer. Ethylene is the smallest unit of polyethylene. Styrene is the smallest unit of polystyrene.

monomorphic bands   DNA fragments of specific sizes found in most individuals. Each different size monomorphic fragment is detected by cleaving genomic DNA with a specific restriction enzyme and hybridizing with a specific monomorphic probe. These fragments provide excellent markers for use in quality control especially as related to band shift.

monozygotic   Twins produced from a single zygote which later splits. The genomes are, therefore, identical.

morphine   White crystalline alkaloid, slightly soluble in water, alcohol, and ether; highly toxic, narcotic, habit-forming drug.

morphology   The science of form and structure of plants and animals, as distinct from consideration of functions.

mosaic   An individual composed of two genetically different cell lines originally derived from the same zygote.

movement   An important element of handwriting. It embraces all the factors related to the motion of the writing instrument-skill, speed, freedom, hesitation, rhythm, emphasis, tremor, and the like. The manner in which the writing instrument is moved, that is, by finger, hand, or arm action, may influence each of these factors.

mtDNA   Maternally inherited mitochondrial DNA. and is present in 1,000 to 10,000 copies per mammalian cells.

mitochondrion   A DNA-containing cytoplasmic organelle of eukaryotes. Mitochrondia are referred to as the powerhouses of the cell because they are site of ATP production.

multi-allele   Refers to a number of different possible alleles at a specific locus.

multilocus   Refers to a number of different possible loci or positions in the genome.

multifactorial trait   A trait characterized by genetic as well as nongenetic factors.

multilocus probe   A probe that is capable of detecting more than one locus at a time.

musket   A firearm with a long barrel and forend or fore-arm extending nearly to the muzzle.

mutagens   Increase the rate of mutation by inducing changes in DNA.

mutation   Any change in the sequence of genomic DNA. This may result from one or many base pair changes. A change in a gene resulting in the formation of another allele.

mutation frequency   The frequency at which a particular mutant is found in the population.

mutation rate   The number of mutation events per gene per unit of time; for example, per cell generation.

N

nanogram (ng)   One billionth (10^9) of a gram.

nanometer   A unit of length equal to one-billionth of a meter, or 10^9 meters.

naphtha   An ambiguous term which may mean high flash naphtha (mineral spirits), or low flash naphtha (petroleum ether, low boiling ligroin) or something altogether different. Flash points and explosive limits vary. The term naphtha is so ambiguous that it should not be used.

narcotic   Pharmacologically, is any substance that produces narcosis: a stuporous state resembling sleep, and characterized by loss of sensation.

natural fibers   A class of fibers of vegetable (e.g. cotton, flax, ramie), animal origin (e.g., silk, wool, and specially furs) or mineral origin (e.g., asbestos).

natural gas   A mixture of low-molecular weight hydrocarbons obtained in petroleum producing regions throughout the world. Natural gas consists of approximately 85% methane, 10% ethane and the balance propanes, butanes and nitrogen. Since it is nearly odorless, an odorizing agent is added to most natural gas prior to final sale.

natural variation   Normal or usual deviations found between repeated specimens of any individual's handwriting or in the product of any typewriter or other record making machines.

natural writing   Any specimen of writing executed normally without an attempt to control or alter its identifying habits and its usual quality of execution. It is the typical writing of an individual.

NEAFS   Northeast Association of Forensic Scientists.

nebulizer   To form a mist of fine droplets from a liquid. To atomize.

negative   The developed film that contains a reversed-tone image of the original scene.

neurogenetics   Study of relationship between genetics and neurology.

neurotoxin   A poisonous substance in snake venom that acts as a nervous system depressant.

neutralize   To make a solution neutral (neither acidic nor basic, pH of 7) by adding a base to an acidic solution, or an acid to a basic solution.

neutral mutation   Any change in the sequence of genomic DNA that does not affect the physical make-up of the individual.

ninhydrin (triketohydrindene hydrate)   A strong oxidizing agent and causes the oxidative deamination of the (α-amino function. The products of the reaction are the resulting aldehyde, ammonia, carbon dioxide, and hydrindantin, a reduced derivative of ninhydrin. The ammonia produced in this way can react with the hydrindantin and another molecule of ninhydrin to yield a purple product.

nitrate   To treat or combine with nitric acid or a compound; to change into a nitro derivative.

nitrite   A salt of nitrous acid.

nitrocellulose   Pulpy, cotton-like, amorphous solid (dry); colorless liquid to semisolid (solution). Used for fast-drying automobile lacquers; high explosives; and leather finishing.

nitrogen   A gaseous element which makes up approximately 80% of the Earth's atmosphere. Nitrogen is relatively inert and does not support either combustion or life. Nitrogen is usually found in the molecular N_2 form.

noise   Any signal generated by the detector not directly responding to the light transmitted at the required wavelength.

non-aqueous ink   Ink in which the pigment or dye is carried in any vehicle other than water. Inks of this class are found in ball point pens, typewriter ribbons, and stamp pads, and are widely used in the printing industry.

non-polymorphic probe   Also known as a *monomorphic probe*. Its sequence is complementary to all human DNA and does not have alternative forms or alleles.

non-secretor   An individual who does not secrete the appropriate A, B, or H group specific substances in the body fluid.

nordiazepam   The active metabolite of diazepam.

normal lens   A lens that makes the image in a photograph appear in perspective similar to that of the original scene. A normal lens has a shorter focal length and a wider field of view than a telephoto lens, and a longer focal length and narrower field of view than a wide-angle lens.

normal-phase chromatogram   Adsorption in which the stationary phase is polar in relation to the mobile phase.

normality (N)   Measure of the number of gram-equivalent weights of a compound per liter of solution.

normal saline   U.S. Pharmacopoeia title for a sterile solution of sodium chloride in purified water, containing 0.9 gram of sodium chloride in 100 milliliters; isotonic with body fluids. Also known as *isotonic sodium chloride solution.*

nortriptyline The mono-N-desmethyl metabolite of amitriptyline and is itself an active antidepressant agent.

nuclear magnetic resonance (NMR) A phenomenon exhibited by a large number of atomic nuclei, in which in a static magnetic field absorb energy from a radio-frequency field at certain characteristic frequencies.

nuclease An enzyme that can degrade DNA by breaking its phosphodiester bonds.

nucleolytic Reactions involve the hydrolysis of a phosphodiester bond in a nucleic acid.

nucleosidase An enzyme that catalyzes the hydrolysis of a nucleoside to its component pentose and its purine or pyrimidine base.

nucleoside A nitrogen base bound to a sugar molecule.

nucleotide(s) A molecule composed of a nitrogen base, a sugar, and a phosphate group; the basic building block of nucleic acids. A building block of DNA or RNA.

nucleotide pair A pair of nucleotides (one in each strand of DNA) that are joined by hydrogen bonds.

nucleus The genome-containing (membrane-bound) structure of eukaryotic organisms.

Numrich Arms Corporation A firearms manufacturer.

nylon A manufactured fiber in which the fiber-forming substance in any long-chain synthetic polyamide in which less than 85% of the amide linkage are attached directly to two aromatic rings.

nylon membrane Nylon paper onto which the DNA is transferred during the Southern blotting procedure.

O

O.F. Mossberg   A firearms manufacturer

objective   The first lens, lens system, or mirror through which light passes or from which it is reflected in an optical system.

oblique lighting examination   An examination with the illumination so controlled that it grazes or strikes the surface of the document from one side at a very low angle, also referred to as a side light examination.

oblique angle   An angle other than perpendicular or parallel.

obliteration/obliterated   Mostly used to referring to serial numbers which are no longer readable. The blotting out or smearing over of writing to make the original invisible or undecipherable.

octane   **1.** An alkane having the formula C_8H_{18}. Flash point of 56°F. Explosive limits of 1% to 3.2%. **2.** A measure of the resistance of a sample of gasoline to premature ignition (knocking). 100 octane fuel has the knocking resistance of 100% iso-octane (2,2,4-trimethyl pentane). Zero-octane fuel has the knocking resistance of n-heptane; 89-octane fuel has the knocking resistance of a mixture of 89% iso-octane and 11% n-heptane.

off-its-feet   The condition of a typeface printing heavier on one side or corner than the remainder of its outline.

offset printing (lithographic)   Printing from a smooth surface plate that has been treated so that the printing areas are ink attracting and the nonprinting areas are ink repelling. Originally this process used a smooth stone surface, but today most offset printing is prepared from specially treated zinc or paper plates.

olefin　　An alkene. An organic compound similar to an alkane, but containing at least one double bond. Olefins have the formula CnH_2n. The simplest olefin is ethylene, C_2H_4.

oligonucleotide　　A polymer composed of a few, usually less than 100, nucleotides. Oligonucleotides are usually synthesized by automated machinery and used as primers in the PCR and as probes.

opacity　　The optical density of a material, usually a pigment; the opposite of transparency. A colorant or paint of high opacity is said to have good hiding power or covering power, by which is meant its ability to conceal another tint or shade over which it is applied.

opaque　　Impervious to light; not translucent. Having no luster; dull.

opiates　　Natural, semisyntheic, or synthetic substances with morphine-like effects in the body. They are primarily employed as analgesics and can be considered narcotic in their effects.

opinion　　In legal language, the document examiner's conclusion. Actually, in court he not only expresses an opinion but demonstrates the reasons for arriving at it.

opium　　A highly toxic plant alkaloid. A habit-forming narcotic, source of morphine.

optical analysis　　Study of properties of a substance or medium, such as its chemical composition or the size of particles suspended in it, through observation of effects on transmitted light, such as scattering, absorption, refraction, and polarization.

optical microscope   An instrument used to obtain an enlarged image of a small object, utilizing visible light; in general its consists of a light source, a condenser, an objective lens, and an ocular or eyepiece, which can be replaced by a recording device. Also known as a *light microscope*.

organic chemistry   The study of the carbon atom and the compounds it forms, mainly with the 20 lightest elements, especially hydrogen, oxygen and nitrogen. Some 3 million organic compounds have been identified and named.

origin   The location of the applied sample or the starting point for the chromatographic development of the applied sample.

origin, point of   The location from which the blood that produced a bloodstain originated. This is determined by projecting angles of impact of well-defined bloodstains back to an axis constructed through the point of convergence.

overdose   An excessive dose of medicine.

overexposure   A condition in which too much light reaches the film, producing a dense negative or a very light print or slide.

ovum   Female gamete or egg cell.

oxidation   Originally, oxidation meant a chemical reaction in which oxygen combines with another substance. The usage of the word has been broadened to include any reaction in which electrons are transferred. The substance which gains electrons is the oxidizing agent.

oxygen   A gaseous element which makes up approximately 20% of the earth's atmosphere. It is usually found in the molecular O_2 form. Oxygen is the most abundant element on earth.

P

packed column   A metal tube evenly filled with a solid support material which is coated with a liquid stationary phase of low vapor pressure.

paint chemistry

> **paint** — a suspension pigment in an oil vehicle. It applies to virtually any surface coating designed for protection of a surface or for decoration, or both. Sometimes the word paint may be a general term and the term "surface coating" is more specific.

> **vehicle** — the portion of a surface coating other than the pigment, the purpose of which is to enable the pigment to be distributed over the surface. The vehicle includes solvents, binders, and other additives. The term vehicle is frequently used to indicate the oil or resin which forms a continuous film and binds the pigment to the substrate.

> **lacquer** — fast-drying coatings, clear or pigment, that dry by evaporation of the solvent rather than by oxidation or polymerization.

> **varnish** — a homogenous solution of drying oils and resins in organic solvents. The resins may be naturally occurring, for example, rosin or dammar, or synthetic, for example, products of the reaction of phenol and formaldehyde.

> **stain** — a solution of a dye or a suspension of a pigment in a vehicle designed to impart a color to wood surface rather than to form a protective coating.

enamel — the term enamel does not intimate the chemical nature of the coating, but implies a pigmented coating which dries to a hard gloss. Increasingly, the term has come to mean a cross-linked thermosetting resin.

latex — a suspension of a pigment in a water-based emulsion of any of several resins, for example, acrylic polymers, vinyl polymers, or styrene-butadiene polymers.

pigment — a finely powdered solid which is essentially insoluble in the medium in which is dispersed. Pigments may be inorganic, such as titanium dioxide, or organic, such as phthalocyanine. White pigments are primarily intended to hide the underlying surface. A pigment is distinguished from a dye in that a dye is soluble in the vehicle while a pigment is not.

drier — a material that promotes or accelerates the drying, curing, or hardening or oxidazable coating vehicles. The principal driers are metal soaps of a monocarboxylic acid.

extender — a low cost white inorganic pigment used with other white pigment to modify the gloss, texture, viscosity, and other properties, and to reduce the cost of the finished product.

solvent — organic liquids of various types having the function of dissolving the binder and thereby providing a consistency to the coating which is more suitable for application.

drying oils — naturally occurring triglycerides which form films principally by air oxidation. The same oils may be used as feedstocks for varnishes, alkyd resins, epoxy ester resins, oil modified urethane resins, and some plasticizers.

plasticizer — a material incorporated into a polymer to increase its flexibility or workability.

thermoplastic polymer — a resin which polymerizes without the necessity of heat. If the resin is heated below its decomposition temperature it softens and hardens again upon cooling; hence, the term thermoplastic.

thermosetting polymer — a resin which can be made to form cross-linkages when baked.

binder — the actual film-former which binds the pigment particles to one another and to the substrate.

palindrome   a DNA site where the base order in one strand is the reverse of that in the complementary strand, for example, 5′GAATTC3′, 3′CTTAAG5′.

palmar zone   the elevated area just behind the fingers and above the center of the palm. Papillary ridges (friction ridges) The fingerprint ridges, which can be observed on the inner surfaces of the hand. Friction ridged skin is a highly specialized organ and differs from the skin on the rest of the body in more than simply its ridged appearance. It has no hair follicles and, thus, no apocrine or sebaceous glands. These ridges occur in certain definite formations, and they can be classified into specific types of patterns.

parabellum   "For war" in Latin. Used in cartridge designations, i.e., 9-mm parabellum

paraffin   A translucent, waxy, solid mixture of hydrocarbons, indifferent to most chemical reagents; it is a constituent of peat, soft coal, and shale, but is derived principally from the distillation of petroleum.

parent drop   A drop of blood from which a wave castoff or satellite spatter originates.

particle theory   Radiation appears to consist of a series of discrete packets of energy (photons).

patching   Retouching or going back over a defective portion of a writing stroke. Careful patching is a common defect in forgeries.

patent   Documented exclusive legal right to a process.

paternity   Refers to the biological father of an offspring.

paternity index (PI)   The ratio of the probability (x) that the putative father is the biological father to the probability (y) that any random man is the biological father. $PI = x + y$.

pathlength   The distance the light passes through the sample.

pathogen   An organism that causes disease in another organism.

pathology   The study of the causes, nature, and effects of diseases and other abnormalities.

pattern   The distribution of a series of shots fired from one gun or a battery of guns under conditions as nearly identical as possible, the points of impact of the projectiles being dispersed about a point called the center of impact.

pattern area   The area which displays the patterns of the fingerprint and is surrounded by the type lines.

PCP   Phencyclidine.

PCR (polymerase chain reaction)   A technique in which cycles of denaturation, annealing with primer, and extension with DNA polymerase, are used to amplify the number of copies of a target DNA sequence more thatn a millionfold using thermal stable Taq polymerase. Oligonucleotide primers must be annealed to the target DNA sequence 5′ flanking regions. The PCR may be likened to a molecular copy machine.

pedigree A "family tree," drawn with standard genetic symbols, showing inheritance patterns for specific phenotypic characters.

pellet 1. The button of particulate material formed after a suspension has been centrifuged. 2. In firearms, a pellet is a common name for the smooth, spherical projectiles loaded in shotshells. Also known as *shot*.

pen Any writing instrument used to apply inks to the paper.

pen emphasis The act of intermittently forcing the pen against the paper surface with increased pressure. When the pen point has flexibility this emphasis produces shading, but with more rigid writing points such as ball point pens heavy pen emphasis can occur in writing without any evidence of shading.

pen lift An interruption in a stroke caused by removing the writing instrument from the paper.

pen nib One of two divisions or points that form the writing portion of a dip pen or fountain pen.

pen position The relationship between the pen point and the paper. Specifically, the angle between the nibs of the pen and the line of writing and between the pen point and the paper surface are the elements of pen position. Both conditions may be reflected in the writing, but is not always revealed except when writing was prepared with a nib pen.

pen pressure The average force with which the pen contacts the paper, as estimated from an examination of the writing. Pen pressure as opposed to pen emphasis, deals with the usual or average force involved in the writing rather than with the periodic increases.

pencil A writing instrument in which the marking portion consists of a compressed stick of graphite or colored marking substance usually mixed with clays and waxes.

pencil grade   A qualitative description of the hardness or softness of a pencil, that is, how dark a stroke it is capable of making.

pencil lead   Not really lead, but a mixture of various types of waxes, clays, graphite, and carbon.

pentane   An alkane having the formula C_5H_{12}, flash point of -40°F, and explosive limits of 1.4% to 8%. Pentane is frequently used to extract flammable or combustible liquid residues from debris samples.

pentobarbital   A derivative of barbituric acid which produces depression of the central nervous system and consequent sedation. Toxic and habit-forming.

Pep A   Peptidase A.

percentile   A division of the members of a group into 100 parts, for example, a value at the 95th percentile indicates that 95% of the values are below that value.

percussion cap   Small metal cup containing a priming compound used in/on percussion firearms. It is placed on the nipple.

percussion composition   A combination of chemical ingredients that will explode when struck sharply with sufficient energy.

periodicity   Pertaining to DNA, it is the number of base pairs per turn of the double helix.

permanent defect   Any identifying characteristic of a typewriter that cannot be corrected by simply cleaning the typeface or replacing the ribbon. Actually, this term in not absolutely accurate, since all defects in typewriters undergo modification and change with time.

petroleum distillates Byproducts of the refining of crude oil. Low boiling or light petroleum distillates (LPD) are highly volatile mixtures of hydrocarbons. These mixtures are sometimes called ligroin, petroleum ether, or naphtha. LPDs are used as cigarette lighter fluids, as copier fluid, and as solvents. Medium boiling petroleum distillates (MPD) are sometimes known as mineral spirits, and are used as charcoal starters, as paint thinners, as solvents for insecticides and other products, and as lamp oil. High boiling or heavy petroleum distillates (HPD) are combustible liquids such as kerosene and diesel fuel.

PGM Phosphoglucomutase, an enzyme found on the surface of red blood cells.

pH The pH value of an aqueous solution is a number describing its acidity of alkalinity. A number used to represent the acidity or alkalinity of an aqueous solution. pH 7 is neutral. Acids have a pH below 7, the lower the pH, the more acidic the solution. Bases have a pH above 7. The higher the pH, the more basic or alkaline the solution.

pH electrode Membrane-type glass electrode used as the hydrogen-ion sensor of most pH meters; the pH-response electrode surface is a thin membrane made of a special glass.

pH meter An instrument used to measure the degree of acidity or alkalinity of a solution. pH 7 (neutral), pH < 7 (acidic), pH > 7 (alkaline).

phage lambda DNA Viral DNA sometimes used for marker lanes.

Phadebas test A test which is used for the detection of the enzyme amylase which is found in saliva.

phasing/orientation mark or point   The place or point on a target which intersects the straight line generated by the alignment of the front and rear sights of a firearm.

phencyclidine (PCP)   A popular drug of abuse, as well as being a legitimate veterinary tranquilizer.

phenobarbital   White, shining, crystalline powder odorless, stable. Toxic; may have damaging side effects. Used in medicine as a sedative.

phenol (carbolic acid)   A poisonous and caustic organic compound used in the isolation of DNA from cellular proteins.

phenolphthalein   Pale yellow powder; forms an almost colorless solution in neutral or acid solution in presence of alkali, but colorless in the presence of large amount of alkali. Used in dyes, acid-base indicator and in medicine as a laxative.

phenotype   The physical make-up of an individual as defined by genetic and nongenetic factors.

phosphatase   An enzyme that removes phosphate groups from substrates.

phosphodiesterases   A class of nucleases, because the reaction that they catalyze is the cleavage of phosphodiester bonds by H_2O.

phosphoglucomutase (PGM)   Among the first genetically polymorphic enzymes to be studied by electrophoresis.

photocopy   A reproduction of a document made on paper by any office or commercial system.

photograph   A reproduction made with a camera and light-sensitive material. The process normally requires two steps: the preparation of a negative on film and the printing of the final positive from it.

photographic negative A transparency produced when black-and-white film is exposed in a camera and then developed. The term is derived from the appearance of the transparency, in which white areas of the original appear the darkest or most opaque, while the darkest portions of the original are almost clear. With color film the light-dark reversal is coupled with a change of colors to the complements of those in the original material.

photograph positive A print made by passing light through the negative generally onto photographic paper. In this print the tonal values are directly proportional to those of the original, that is, light areas of the original appear light, and dark areas dark.

photography To write or draw with light. Recording with light is closer to the modern meaning of the word.

photoionization detector (PID) A type of detector used in chromatography which employs ultraviolet radiation rather than a flame to ionize compounds as they pass through a detector. Photoionization detectors are particularly sensitive to aromatic compounds.

photomicrographs A photograph made through a compound microscope and may be a greatly enlarged image of a small area. A similarly enlarged photograph may be prepared with only a lens of very short focal length and is accurately termed a photomacrograph. It is extremely difficult to distinguish between photographs made by the two processes, and both are often incorrectly referred to as a photomicrograph.

Photostat® A commercial reproduction in which a negative copy, white writing on a black background, is made directly on photosensitive paper. The process employs a special camera equipped with a lens and inverting prism. The inverting prism causes the writing in the negative copy to run from left to right, i.e., in the same direction as in the original rather than backward. A photostatic positive, that is black writing on a white background, must be prepared by rephotostating the negative copy. The method is obsolete and has been replaced by various dry photocopying methods.

picroindigocarmine solution   A greenish stain which is used in conjunction with Kernechtrot solution for the identification of human sperm. The solution will stain the tail of the sperm a greenish-blue color.

pigment   A finely divided insoluble material used to deluster or color fibers (e.g., titanium dioxide, iron oxide).

pipette   A small tube, often graduated, for removing small portions of a fluid and can be used for measuring the volume of liquids.

pistol (automatic, semi-automatic, single shot)   A small firearm having a stock that fits in the hand and has a short barrel.

pitch   The number of crowns per inch of the same strand.

plaintiff   The complaining party in a litigation.

plane polarized light   Light that is vibrating in one plane.

plasma   The fluid portion of unclotted blood.

plasma membrane   The continuous membrane defining the boundary of every cell.

plasmid   An autonomous self-replicating extrachromosomal circular DNA.

plastic prints   Is actually an indentation. This type of pattern is formed by pressing the friction ridges of the fingers onto a soft surface, such as wax, putty, tar, soap, butter, or clay. They are usually photographed and sometimes may be cast.

platinum chloride   The platinum chloride of commerce is usually chloroplatinic acid. A brown solid or red crystal; soluble in water and alcohol, used as a chemical reagent.

platen   The cylinder that serves as the backing for the paper and absorbs the blow from the typeface.

plectonemic winding   Describes the interwining of the two strands in the classical double helix of DNA.

pleiotropic   Genes affects more than one (apparently unrelated) characteristic of the phenotype.

pleochroism   The property exhibited by double-refracting colored crystals of showing different colors when the transmitted light is viewed along different axes. The color depends on the orientation of the substance and arises because of differential absorption of light in the different orientations.

ploidy   Refers to the number of copies of the chromosome set present in a cell; a haploid has one copy, a dipoid has two copies, ect.

ply   The number of single yarn twisted together to form a piled cord; an individual yarn in a plied yarn or cord.

poach   The illegal taking of wildlife.

point of convergence   A point to which a bloodstain pattern can be projected. This point is determined by tracing the long axis of well-defined bloodstains within the pattern back to a common point or source.

point mutation   changes involving single base pairs.

polarity   The measure of an electrical charge on a molecule. Most flammable or combustible liquids are nonpolar. Many water-soluble compounds, including alcohols and acetone, are polar.

polarized light (nicol)   An optical material (Iceland spar) that function as a prism,separating light rays that pass through it into two portions, one of which is reflected away, and the other transmitted. The transmitted portion is called plane-polarized light.

polarized light microscope (PLM)   A refined biological microscope stands to which several special purpose features have been added. These features should include, at minimum, a polarizer, an analyzer, a rotatable circular stage, a cross-hair ocular, and a compensator slot. Quarter- and full-wave compensators should be part of the standard equipment. The availability of at least one variable compensator is also highly desirable.

polyacrylamide   A material used to make electrophoretic gels for separation of mixtures of macromolecules.

polyacrylamide gel electrophoresis (PAGE)   Used to identify size differences in VNTRs.

polyA tail   The adenine nucleotide polymer attached to the 3′ end of pre-mRNA.

polyester fiber   A synthetic fiber of high tensile strength made by the esterification of ethylene glycol and other organic compounds.

polyethylene terephthalate   A polyester formed from ethylene glycol by direct esterification or by catalyzed ester exchange between ethylene glycol and dimethyl terephthalate. Uses: blended with cotton, for wash-and-wear fabrics, blended with wool, for worsteds and suitings; packaging films; recording tapes.

polygonal rifling   Helical grooves in the bore of a firearm barrel to impart rotary motion to a projectile.

polymarkers (PM)   Multiple loci examined in PCR. (Five loci are combined in a commercially available DNA typing kit).

polymer   A large molecule consisting of repeating units of a monomer. Polymers may be natural, such as cellulose, or synthetic, such as most plastics. A compound composed of many smaller subunits; results from the process of polymerization.

polymerase   An enzyme believed to catalyze the formation of messenger DNA in the cell.

polymerization   A chemical reaction, usually carried out with a catalyst, heat, or light, in which two or more relatively simple molecules (monomers) combine to form a chainlike macromolecule, or polymer. When comprised of two monomers a polymer is called a dimer; of three, a trimer; of four, a tetramer.

polymorphic probe   A known DNA sequence that recognize a locus that is polymorphic.

polymorphism   Refers to the simultaneous occurrence in the population of genomes showing allelic variation (as seen either in alleles producing different phenotypes or, for example, in changes in DNA affecting the restriction pattern). A section of the DNA that varies greatly from person to person.

polypeptide   A long chain of amino acids linked by peptide bonds, a protein.

polypropylene (C_3H_5)n   A synthetic crystalline thermoplastic polymer, with molecular weight of 40,000 or more.

population genetic   The study of the frequency of genes and alleles in various populations.

pores in gel   Tiny comb-like holes in an agarose gel designed to slow the movement of DNA fragments during electrophoresis.

positive   The opposite of a negative; an image with the same tonal relationships as those in the original scene e.g., a finished print or slide.

positive control   Those samples when run in a chemical reaction give a positive result. Those samples give the same result each time.

potassium chlorate ($KClO_3$)   Transparent, colorless crystals or white powder, used as a oxidizing agent, explosives, matches, percussion caps, and textile printing.

potassium ferricyanide ($K_3Fe(CN)_6$ Bright red, lustrous crystals or powder. Used for tempering steel; etching liquid; production of pigments; electroplating and fertilizer compositions.

potassium nitrate (KNO_3)   Transparent, colorless or white crystalline powder or crystals. Used in pyrotechnics; explosives; matches; metallurgy and glass manufacture.

potassium oxalate ($K_2C_2O_4.H_2O$)   Colorless transparent crystals. Odorless; soluble in water. and highly toxic if inhaled or ingested. Strong irritant to tissue. Used to remove stains from textiles and photography.

potassium perchlorate ($KClO_4$)   Colorless crystals or white, crystalline powder. Decomposed by concussion, organic matter, and agents subject to oxidation. Used in explosives; medicine; oxidizing agent; photography; pyrotechnics and flares.

potassium permanganate ($KMnO_4$)   Dark-purple crystals; blue metallic sheen; sweetish astringent taste; odorless. Used as a oxidizer; disinfectant; deodorizer;

dye tanning; radioactive decontamination of skin and reagent in analytical chemistry.

powder (smokeless or black powder)   A finely ground or comminuted mass of free particles formed from a solid substance in the dry state; dust. An explosive dry powder, as gunpowder.

precipitant   Any substance, as a reagent, that when added or applied to a solution results in the formation of a precipitate.

precipitate   A substance separating, in solid particles, from a liquid as the result of a chemical or physical change.

precipitin   An antibody produced in the blood serum by inoculation with foreign protein and capable of providing immunity against specific bacteria.

precision   A measure of reproducibility of a test result.

prehybridization   The process of incubating a DNA blot with a hybridization solution to, in part, block cross-reactive sites. This precedes the addition of labeled probe.

primer DNA   A short, perhaps 20-mer, oligonucleotide annealed to the 5' end of a DNA template. The primer provides an initiation point for addition of deoxyribonucleotides in DNA replication.

print   A positive picture, usually on paper, and usually produced from a negative; (M) a copy of a motion picture.

probability   A statistical means of describing uncertainty.

probe   A specific sequence of DNA that attaches to unzipped DNA. A single-stranded segment of DNA, or mRNA, capable of being tagged with a tracer, such as ^{32}P, and hybridized to its complementary sequence.

processing (also M)   Developing, fixing, and washing exposed photographic film or paper to produce either a negative image or a positive image.

product gel   Is used as a tool to assess the efficiency of amplification by Tag polymerase.

product rule   A liberal method of calculating population frequency of alleles across multiple loci that are not linked.

proficiency testing   A test designed to evaluate the ablility of an analyst an/or laboratory to perform certain analyses.

programming   A method of gas chromatographic analysis which reproducibly raises the temperature of the column so as to allow better resolution of the components over a wide range of boiling points.

projected blood pattern   A pattern created when a force other than a low-velocity impact acts upon a quantity of blood approximately 0.10 ml or greater.

projection prints   A print made by focusing light from the negative on the printing paper by means of a lens system. These positives are generally enlargements. Some workers refer to them as "bromides" because of the type of paper emulsion originally used.

prokaryote   A unicellular organism lacking a membrane-bound nucleus, for example, bacteria. Prokaryotes do not undergo mitosis.

proofload, provisional proof (historical)   A cartridge loaded to specified pressures higher than service loads to test firearms barrels during manufacture, but before assembly; sometimes called a *"blue pill."*

proof mark   A stamp applied at or near the breech of a firearm after it has passed a proof test.

proof test The firing of a deliberate overload to test the strength of a firearm barrel and/or action.

proximal Relatively nearer to central portion of the body or point of origin.

propane An alkane having the formula C_3H_8. Propane is the major constituent of LP gas. Explosive limits of 2.4% to 9%. One cubic foot a propane has a heating value of 2500 BTU.

proportion The fraction or percent of individuals or measurements in a specific subgroup of the total group under consideration.

proportional-spacing typewriter A modern form of typewriting resembling printing in that letters, numerals, and symbols do not occupy the same horizontal space as they do with a conventional typewriter. For example, the "i" occupies two units, the "o" three, and the "m" five.

propoxyphene A mildly effective narcotic analgesic, somewhat less potent than codeine, that bears a close structural relationship to methadone.

protein The agents of biological function; they are also the expressions of genetic information. A biological molecule composed of amino acids. Protein serves as the "building blocks" of body structures or as the enzymes that initiate specific biochemical reactions.

proteinase K A hydrolytic enzyme used in the digestion of proteins to amino acids.

protocol The original record made of the results of a test.

pseudocumene (1,2,4-trimethyl benzene) A component of gasoline.

pump action   A firearm which features movable forearm which is manually actuated in motion parallel to the barrel by the shooter. Also known as "slide action."

putative father   A man accused but not proven to be the biological father of an offspring.

pyridine   A colorless liquid, nitrogenous compound, C_5H_5N, with a pungent, noxious odor. Used in organic syntheses, as a disinfectant, antiseptic, and alcohol denaturant.

pyrimidine   An organic compound, $C_4H_4N_2$, resulting from the acid hydrolysis of a nucleic acid. A type of nitrogen base; the pyrimidine bases in DNA are cytosine and thymine.

prying tool   A tool which can be used to forcibly open a locked door/cover by applying leverage to the door/cover at one of its edges.

pyrolysis   Decomposition by the application of or as a result of heat. The breaking apart of complex molecules into simpler units by the use of heat, as in the pyrolysis of heavy oil to make gasoline.

pyrophoric distillation   The slow drying and passive pyrolysis of wood materials.

Q

qualification   The professional experience, education, and ability of an analysts to perform his duties. Before he is permitted to testify as an expert witness, the court must rule that he is a qualified expert in his field.

quality assurance   Controls and checks that aid in assuring the reliability of the experimental process.

quality audit   A systematic and independent examination and evaluation to determine whether quality activities and results comply with planned arrangements and whether these arrangements are implemented effectively and are suitable to achieve objectives.

quality control (QC)   A monitoring system to ensure assay results adhere to appropriate precision and accuracy levels.

quality plan   A document setting out the specific quality practices, resources, and activities relevant to a particular product, process, service contract, or project.

Quantiblot®   A slot blot technique that is used to obtain information about the quantity of human DNA recovered from a sample.

quantitative inheritance   Inheritance of measurable traits (height, weight, color intensity) that depend on the cumulative action of many genes, each producing a small effect on the phenotype.

questioned document   Any document about which some issue has been raised or that is under scrutiny.

questioned (sample)   Material collected as or from items of evidence which have a known location but an unknown originating source.

quinine   Bulky, white, amorphous powder or crystalline alkaloid; very bitter taste; odorless and levorotatory. Used in medicine as antimalarial drug.

R

race As applied to the human species (Homo sapiens), a population subgroup with a gene pool characteristic only of that group.

radioactive DNA DNA, usually a probe in RFLP testing, that is tagged with radioactive phosphorous.

radiation **1.** Transfer of heat through electromagnetic waves from hot to cold. **2.** Electromagnetic waves of energy having frequency and wavelength. The shorter wavelengths (higher frequency) are more energetic. The electromagnetic spectrum is comprised of gamma rays, X-rays, visible light rays, infrared, microwave, and radio waves, cosmic rays and ^{32}P ultraviolet rays.

radionuclide A radioactive element. ^{32}P (radioactive phosphorus) is a high-energy β-nuclide.

random "man" Any individual in the population whose DNA profile matches a crime specimen profile or an offspring's paternally derived profile.

rape Sexual intercourse between a man and a woman without the woman's consent. This may occur by deception or by force.

rate of twist The distance required for the rifling to complete one revolution.

reading frame The DNA codon sequence transcribed into pre-mRNA.

reagent blank control This control consists of all reagents used in the test process minus any sample. This is used to detect DNA contamination of the analytical reagents and materials.

reagent chemicals   High-purity chemicals used for analytical reactions, for testing of new reactions where the effect of impurities are unknown, and in general, for chemical work where impurities must either be absent or at a known concentration.

reannealing   Spontaneous realignment of two single DNA strands to re-form a DNA double helix that had been denatured.

rebound   A defect in which a character prints a double impression with the lighter one slightly offset to the right or left.

recessive   A trait phenotypically expressed only when an abnormal gene is present in the homozygous state.

recessive allele   Is obscured in the phenotype of a heterozygote by the dominant allele, often due to inactivity or absence of the product of the recessive allele.

recombinant   Progency have a different genotype from that of either parent.

recombinant DNA   DNA formed by the union of two heterologous DNA molecules, for example, the ligation of a human growth hormone gene into a plasmid.

recombinant DNA technology   Refers specifically to in vitro ligation of two heterologous DNA molecules, for example, the splicing of a human DNA tandem repeat sequence into plasmid pBR322. As a generalization, the technology refers to the new approach of direct DNA analysis.

recombination   Combinations of genes in offspring different from those in the parents due to independent assortment and crossing over.

reference collection   Material complied and organized by the scientist to assist them in answering specific questions.

refraction   The change in direction observed when light passes obliquely from one medium to another in which it travels with a different velocity.

refractive index (N)   The change in direction (apparent bending) of a light ray passing from one medium to another of different density, as from air to water or glass. The ratio of the sine of the angle of incidence to the sine of the angle of refraction is the index of refraction of the second medium. Index of refraction of a substance may also be expressed as the ration of the velocity of light in a vacuum to its velocity in the substance.

rehybridized membrane   A nylon membrane from which a DNA probe is removed (stripped) and hybridized to a second DNA probe.

Remington Arms   A firearms manufacturer.

renaturation   The reassociation of denatured complementary single strands of a DNA double helix. The restoration of a molecule to its native form. Repeating unit In a tandem cluster is the length of the sequence that is repeated; appears circular on a restriction map.

repetitious DNA   DNA consisting of repeated chromosomal nucleotide sequence.

repetition frequency   The (integral) number of copies of a given sequence present in the haploid genome; equal 1 for nonrepetitive DNA, >2 for repetitive DNA.

repetitious sequence   A repeated series of bases in a DNA molecule.

replicon   A unit of the genome in which DNA is replicated; contains an origin for initiation of replication.

resolution   **1.** In chromatography, a measure of the separation of components. Also, the ability to visually separate two spots. **2.** In spectroscopy, a measure of the ability of the instruments to detect individual absorbance peaks.

resolving power   The maximum number of distinguishable lines per millimeter that can be recorded by photographic material or by a lens. Not all photographic materials or lenses have the same characteristics in this respect.

restoration   Any process in which erased writing is developed or brought out again on the document itself.

restriction endonuclease   Enzymes (molecular scissors) that cleave double-stranded DNA at specific palindromic base recognition sequences. The sequences are usually different for each enzyme. Restriction enzymes are named according to the bacterial species of origin.

restriction enzyme   An enzyme that cuts DNA internally at a specific, known sequence site.

restriction fragment length polymorphism (RFLP)
The different length fragments of DNA produced by the action of a restriction enzyme at a specific polymorphic site. If the restriction endonuclease recognizes the variable site, then two fragments are produced; if not, only one is formed. An individual may be homozygous or heterozygous, that is, the site may be present or absent on both chromosomes of the homologous pair, or it may be present on one and absent on the other. It should also be noted that different fragment lengths are produced if distance between the fixed recognition sites changes. This can occur because of the insertion or deletion of nucleotides or because of a variable number of tandem repeats.

restriction map   A linear array of sites on DNA cleaved by various restriction enzymes.

retardation (r)   The actual distance of one of the doubly refracted rays behind the other as they emerge from an anisotropic fiber. Dependent upon the difference in the two refractive indices, $n_2 - n_1$ and the thickness of the fiber.

retardation factor (RF)   The ratio of the distance traveled by the solute spot's center divided by the distance traveled by the solvent front, both measured from the origin.

retention index   In gas chromatography, the relationship of retention volume with arbitrarily assigned numbers to the compound being analyzed; used to indicate the volume retention behavior during analysis.

retention time   The length of time required for a compound or component of a mixture to pass through a chromatographic column.

retracing   Any stroke that goes back over another writing stroke. In natural handwriting there may be many instances in which the pen doubles back over the same course, but some retracing in fraudulent signatures represent a reworking of a letter form or stroke.

revolver   A type of pistol with a revolving cylinder in the breech chambered to hold several cartridges so that it may be fired in succession without reloading.

Rhesus factor (Rh factor)   Any of a group of genetically transmitted agglutinogens present in the blood of most individuals (Rh positive), and those individuals without the factor are referred to as Rh negative.

rhythm   The element of the writing movement marked by regular or periodic recurrences. It may be classed as smooth, intermittent, or jerky in its quality.

ribbon condition
Cloth or multiple-use typewriter ribbons gradually deteriorate with use, and the degree of deterioration is a measure of the ribbon condition.

ribbon impression   Typewriting made directly through a cloth or carbon film ribbon is called a ribbon impression. Original typewriting is made in this way.

ribonucleic acid (RNA)   Single-stranded nucleic acid molecules composed of the ribonucleosides adenosine, guanosine, cytidine, and uridine. The three types of RNA include mRNA, rRNA, and tRNA.

ricochet   The deflection of a projectile(s) after impact.

ridge characteristics

1. bifurcation (fork) — This is a single ridge, splitting or forking into two branches.

2. island (enclosure) — An island is formed by a single ridge which, after bifurcating for a short distance, reconverges and continues as a single ridge. An enclosure usually refers to a larger island.

3. dot — A dot is a very short ridge and means exactly what the word dot implies.

4. short ridge — A relative term, and is used to denote a ridge that is not as long as the average ridge in that specific print.

5. ridge ending — The point of the ridge's termination. It is considered an ending ridge only if it terminates within the pattern area.

6. trifurcation — This is one single ridge splitting into a three-pronged, fork-shaped pattern.

7. bridge — A bridge is a short ridge which interconnects two other parallel ridges.

8. angle — An angle results from two or more ridges converging with one another at a point.

9. converging ridges — Two or more ridges which meet at a point are converging, and the point at which they meet is called the point of convergence.

10. diverging ridges — Diverging ridges are ridges which are parallel for some distance but then swing out away from each other.

rifle   A firearm having rifling in the bore and designed to be fired from the shoulder.

rifled slug   A single projectile with spiral grooves and hollow base, intended for use in shotguns. The theory of the grooves is that after leaving the gun barrel's muzzle the slug will rotate and thus reach its target much more accurately.

rifling methods

1. broach, gang — a tool having a series of cutting edges of slightly increasing height used to cut the spiral grooves in a barrel.

2. broach, single — a non-adjustable rifling cutter which cuts all of the grooves simultaneously, and is used in a series of increasing dimensions until the desired groove depth is achieved.

3. button — a hardened metal plug, called a button, with a rifled cross section configuration. It is pushed or pulled through a drilled and reamed barrel so as to cold form the spiral grooves to the desired depth and twist. When the carbide button was first introduced it was described as a swaging process or swaged rifling.

4. hook — a cutting tool which has a hook shape and only cuts one groove at a time.

5. scrape — a cutting tool which cuts two opposing grooves at a time.

6. swage — an internal mandrel with rifling configuration which forms rifling in the barrel by means of external hammering. Also known as *hammer forging*.

roller pen   A type of ball-point pen that uses aqueous ink.

S

sample   A selected, representative portion of the whole. Representative fraction of material tested or analyzed in order to determine the nature, composition, and percentage of specified constituents, and possibly their reactivity.

Savage Arms / Savage Anschutz   A firearms manufacturer.

satellite DNA   Consists of many tandem repeats (identical or related) of a short basic repeating unit.

satellite spatter   Small droplets of blood that are projected around or beside a drop of blood upon impact with a surface. A wave castoff us also considered a form of satellite spatter.

saturation   The status in which all available bonds of an atom are attached to other atoms. Alkanes are saturated. Olefins are unsaturated. In thin-layer chromatography, chamber equilibration with mobile phase solvent vapor prior to chromatography.

scheduled quantities   Quantities of radioisotopes as defined in atomic energy control.

scanning   The process where the wavelength range of the system is viewed in order, usually from lowest to highest wavelength.

scanning electron microscope (SEM)   Used to study surface morphology. The images produced are striking and often give the illusion of being three-dimensional.

screening   Preliminary testing.

secret inks   A material used for writing that is not visible until treated by developing process; also referred to as sympathetic ink.

secretor   An individual whose genetic markers can be detected by using their saliva and testing for polymorphic antigen, which adhere to cell surfaces, such as the Lewis system.

secobarbital   A barbiturate derivative of short duration of action, used as either a sedative or hypnotic.

secondary splash or ricochet   The deflection of large volumes of blood after impact with a target surface to another target surface.

self-replication   A duplication process whereby each strand of the DNA double helix acts as a template for replication of its complementary strand.

selvage   The narrow edge of woven fabric that runs parallel to the wrap. It is made with stronger yarns in a tighter construction than the body of the fabric to prevent raveling.

semen   Sperm plus seminal fluid.

seminal fluid   The impregnating fluid of male animals.

sequence of strokes   The order in which writing strokes are placed on the paper.

serologist(s)   An individual who characterizes and identifies blood and body fluids.

serology   The science of serums and their actions.

serrations   The state of being edged as with saw teeth.

serum   Watery fluid which separates from blood on coagulation.

serum stain   A clear, yellowish stain with a shiny surface often appearing around a bloodstain after the blood has retracted due to clotting.

sex chromosomes (X and Y chromosomes)   Are those whose contents are different in the two sexes; usually labeled X and Y, male have XY chromosomes and female have XX chromosomes.

sex-linked characteristic   A pattern of inheritance shown by genes carried on a sex chromosomes (usually the X).

shading   A widening of the ink stroke due to added pressure on a flexible pen point or to the use of a stub pen.

sheared DNA   DNA broken into fragments by mechanical action.

shot   Spherical pellets used in loading shotshells or cartridges.

shot spread   The diameter of a shot pattern.

shotgun   A smooth-bore shoulder firearm designed to fire shotshells containing numerous pellets or sometimes a single projectile.

shotshell   A cartridge containing projectile(s) designed to be fired in a shotgun. The cartridge body may be metal, plastic or paper.

shutter   Blades, a curtain, a plate, or some other movable cover in a camera that controls the time during which light reaches the film.

sidelighting   Light striking the subject from the side relative to the position of the camera; produces shadows and highlights to create modeling on the subject.

sign of elongation   Referring to the elongation of a fiber in relation to refractive indices. If elongation in the direction of the high refractive index, the fiber is said to be positive; if elongation in the direction of the low refractive index, it is said to be negative.

signal   Radioactive emission from a probe attached to DNA on a nylon membrane that causes X-ray film to darken. The darkened areas are called bands and correlate with the location of the probe on the original membrane.

significant writing habit   Any characteristic of handwriting that is sufficiently uncommon and well fixed to serve as a fundamental point in the identification.

silencer   A tubular device attached to the muzzle of a firearm rendering the discharge noiseless.

simulation   The act of simulating; counterfeit; sham.

single-element typewriter   Typewriters using either a type ball or type wheel printing device. The IBM Selectric machine was the first modern typewriter of the group.

single-strand exchange   Is a reaction in which one of the strands of a duplex of DNA leaves its former partner and instead pairs with the complementary strand in another molecule, displacing its homologue in the second duplex.

size marker   DNA fragments of known molecular weight and base pair length, such as λ-phage digested with the restriction enzyme Hind III, run on electrophoresis gels for the determination of DNA sample fragment sizes.

skid marks (slippage marks)   Rifling marks formed on the bearing surface of bullets as they enter the rifling of the barrel before rotation of the bullet starts. Skid marks are typically produced by revolvers and have the appearance of a widening of the land impression at their beginning point.

skill   In any act there are relative degrees of ability or skill, and a specimen of handwriting usually contains evidence of the writer's proficiency.

slant The angle or inclination of the axis of letters relative to the baseline.

slide A photographic transparency mounted for projection.

slit-width Size of the opening of slit through which light emerges. Size depends on wavelength range, separation ability of wavelength selector, and desired isolation of specific wavelength.

slug A term applied to a single projectile for shotshells.

smeared-over writing An obliteration accomplished by covering the original writing with an opaque substance.

Smith & Wesson A firearms manufacturer.

smooth bore A firearm with unrifled bore.

smudge A bloodstain that has been distorted to a degree so that further classification is not possible.

sodium acetate Colorless, odorless crystals, used in dye and color intermediate; soaps, photography, laboratory reagent, and dehydrating agent.

sodium fluoride and potassium oxalate Chemical found inside a gray top test tube, the sodium fluoride prevents bacterial growth and the potassium oxalate bind the calcium in the blood. This the test tube use when testing for alcohol in the blood.

sodium hydroxide The most important commercial caustic. White, deliquescent flakes, crystalline fracture. Chemical manufacture; rayon and cellophane; regenerating ion exchange resins and textile processing.

sodium rhodanate (sodium thiocyanate) Colorless deliquescent crystals or white powder; used as an analytical reagent; dyeing and printing textiles and solvent for polyacrylates.

solute   In thin-layer chromatography, a mixture of components to be separated. The substance dissolved in a solvent.

solution   A single, homogeneous liquid, solid, or gas phase that is a mixture in which the components (liquid, gas, solid) are uniformly distributed throughout the mixture.

solvent   A substance capable of dissolving another substance (solute) to form a uniformly dispersed mixture (solution) at the molecular or ionic size level.

solvent front   The final point reached by the mobile phase as it flows up or across the thin-layer chromatography plate during development of the chromatogram.

somatic cells   All cells of eukaryotes excluding gametes.

Southern blot   The process if transferring DNA fragments from agarose gel to a nylon membrane or cellulose filter, leaving the fragments in the exact position they had in the gel.

Southern blotting   A technique developed by E. Southern for the direct transfer of DNA fragments from an agarose gel onto a solid support such as a nylon membrane. The transfer occurs by salt–solution capillary action.

spalling   Destruction of a surface by frost, heat, corrosion, or mechanical causes. Concrete exposed to intense heat may spall explosively. Expansion and contraction of the concrete as well as vaporizing moisture contained in the concrete contribute to this effect. It does not necessarily mean an accelerant was used.

specificity   The special affinity between an antigen and its corresponding antibody.

spectrometer   Photometric device for the measurement of spectral transmittance, spectral reflectance, or relative spectral emittance. An instrument used to measure the intensity of a specific wavelength of light entering and leaving a solution.

spectrophotometer An instrument used to measure the intensity of a specific wavelength of light entering and leaving a solution. A light-measuring device which incorporates a monochrometer to isolate and project particular wavelengths of electromagnetic radiation through a sample, and a detector to measure the amount of radiation which has passed through the sample.

spectroradiometer A form of spectrometer for determining the distribution of the intensity of any type of radiation especially in the infrared region of the spectrum.

spectroscopy Observation by means of an optical device (spectroscope) of the wavelength and intensity of electromagnetic radiation (light) absorbed or emitted by various materials.

speed of writing Not everyone writes at the same rate, so that consideration of the speed of writing may be a significant identifying element. Writing speed cannot be measured precisely from the finished handwriting but can be interpreted in broad terms as slow, moderate, or rapid.

speer To inquire, ask, or to question.

spermatozoa (sperm) A male reproductive cell. The male fertilizing element of an animal, usually in the form of a nucleated cell with a long flagellate process or tail by which it swims actively about.

spherulites Spheres composed of needles or rods all oriented perpendicular to the outer surface, or a plane section through such a sphere. A common form of polymer crystallization from melts or concentrated solutions.

spine   The pointed edge characteristics that radiate away from the center of a bloodstain. Their formation depends upon impact velocity and surface texture.

spinneret   One of organs perforated by tubes connected with glands secreting liquid silk, in spider. A metal plate pierced with holes through which filaments of plastic material are forced, as in the making of rayon fibers.

spinous   Spinelike; prickly.

splash   A stain pattern created by a low-velocity impact upon a quantity of blood approximately 0.10 ml or greater striking a surface.

splicing   A term used by document examiners to denote the slight overlapping of two strokes after an interruption in the writing. It may be a part of imitated, fraudulent signatures that are prepared one or two letters at a time.

spontaneous heating   Also known as *spontaneous combustion*. Initially, a slow, exothermic reaction at ambient temperatures. Liberated heat, if undissipated (insulated), accumulates at an increasing rate and may lead to spontaneous ignition of any combustibles present. Spontaneous ignition occurs sometimes in haystacks, coal piles, warm moist cotton waste, and in stacks of rags coated with drying oils such as cottonseed or linseed oil.

spot   A round zone of sample application at the origin: or in a chromatogram, a round zone caused by migration of a component of the solute.

spotting   Applying a solute sample at the origin of the thin-layer chromatography plate.

spurious signature   A fraudulent signature in which there was no apparent attempt at simulation or imitation. It is common form of forgery encountered in investigations of fraudulent checks where the person passing the check depends on the surrounding circumstances rather than upon the quality of the signature for his success.

squib load   A cartridge or shell which produces projectile velocity and sound substantially lower than normal. May result in projectile and/or wads remaining in the bore.

SSO   Sequence-specific oligonucleotide.

standards   A condensed and compact set of authentic specimens which, if adequate and proper, should contain a true cross section of the material from a known source.

standard deviation (SD)   A statistical measure of the dispersion of values around a mean.

standard error (SE)   A statistical measure of the dispersion of a series of sample means around the population mean.

standard photograph   Is made of film sizes of 21/4 × 31/4 in. or larger. The negative image is only slightly reduced and more generally is of natural size or enlarged.

stationary phase   The solid adsorbent coating layer on thin-layer chromatography plates. In a packed column, the stationary phase is a low vapor pressure liquid that coats a solid support. Compounds are selectively retained based on their solubility in this liquid. In a capillary column, the stationary phase is generally a modified or unmodified polysiloxane compound coating the walls of a fused silica column. Compounds are selectively retained based on their interaction with the coating's functional group.

statistic   A computed quantity characteristic of a population such as the mean.

statistical analysis   The body of techniques used in statistical inference concerning a population.

statistical distribution   The array of frequencies of different quantitative or qualitative classes in a population.

stereo microscope   An instrument for blending into one image two pictures of an object from slightly different points of view, so as to produce upon the eye the impression of relief and solidity.

sterile technique   Gloves, sterile supplies, and clean work areas are required in addition to the use of separate pipet tips for each reagent addition to each reaction tube.

steroid   One of a group of polycyclic compounds closely related biochemically to terpenes.

STR   Short-tandem repeats; also called *microsatellites*. An elementary form of repetitive DNA occurs in mammalian genomes, determined by di-, tri-, and tetranucleotide repeats arranged in very short arrays.

strand   A single fiber, filament, or monofilament.

striations   Parallel surface contour variations on the surface of an object caused by a combination of force and motion where the motion is approximately parallel to the plane being marked. These striations are accidental in nature and unique to a common origin, (a particular firearm or tool).

stringency   The buffer salt concentration and temperature used in the DNA blot wash posthybridization process. As these parameters are changed, the degree of binding of probe to target DNA changes.

strip removal The melting of hydrogen bonds, of hybridized probe from DNA blots.

structural gene A DNA sequence coding for a specific message.

strychnine An alkaloid found together with the less active brucine in the seeds of *Strychnos nux-vomica*, a tree indigenous to India. It is a potent central nervous stimulant and convulsant, acting by the selective blockage of post-synaptic neuronal inhibition.

styrene (vinylbenzene) An aromatic compound having the formula $C_6H_5C_2H_3$. The monomer of polystyrene plastic. A common product of polymer pyrolysis.

Sturm, Ruger & Co. A firearm manufacturer.

subgeneric class A group of fibers within a generic class which share the same polymer composition. Subgeneric names include, for example, nylon 6, nylon 6,6, and poly(ethylene terephthalate).

subpoena A written command summoning a specific individual to appear in court under penalty for failure to do so.

subpopulation A smaller segment of a related population. Also known as *stratum*.

substrate matrix. The material from which a substance to be analyzed is removed.

substrate control Unstained material adjacent to, or representative of, the area upon which the biological material is deposited.

sulfur A nonmetallic yellow element. A constituent of black powder, sulfur burns readily when in powdered form.

supernatant The liquid portion separated after a suspension is centrifuged.

suppressor gene   A modifying gene which will completely or partially suppress the expression of another gene.

suspect specimen   A specimen obtained from a suspect for analysis.

surface dye   A colorant bound to the surface of a fiber.

surface texture   The surface of any sheet of paper when viewed under magnification is not absolutely smooth and flat, but irregular and rough. Surface texture describes this property.

swipe, smear   The transfer of blood onto a surface not already contaminated with blood. One edge is usually feathered which may indicated the direction of travel.

synthetic dye inks   Any ink consisting simply of a dye dissolved in water together with the necessary preservatives. Various dyes are used in commercial ink manufacture today; the aniline dyes were the first of these, and some writers still refer to inks of this class as aniline inks.

synthetic fibers   A class of manufactured polymeric fibers which are synthesized from chemical compound (e.g. nylon, polyester).

system (of writing)   The combination of the basic design of letters and the writing movement as taught in school. Writing through use diverges from the system, but generally retains some influence of the basic training.

T

T   A single-letter designation of the pyrimindine base, thymine

Takayama test   Used for the identification of blood. Also called *hemochromogen crystals.*

tag   A tracer linked into a molecule, for example, ^{32}P labeling of a DNA probe.

Taq polymerase   A DNA polymerase isolated from the bacterium *Thermus aquaticus* that lives in hot springs. This enzyme is capable of withstanding high temperatures and is, therefore, very useful in the polymerase chain reaction (PCR).

tandem repeats   The end to end duplication of a series of identical or almost identical stretches of DNA.

target   A surface upon which blood has been deposited.

target DNA   The DNA sequence to be hybridized to a specific probe.

tatooing   Small hemorrhagic marks on the skin produced by the impact of gunpowder particles. Also called *stippling.*

technical fiber   A bundle of natural fibers composed of individual elongated cells that can be physically or chemically separated and examined microscopically for identifying characteristics (e.g. hemp, jute, and sisal).

Teichmann test   Used as a confirmatory test for bloodstains. Also called *hemin crystals.*

telephoto lens   A lens that makes a subject appear larger on film than does a normal lens at the same camera-to-subject distance. A telephoto lens has a longer focal length and narrower field of view than a normal lens.

telogen   A quiescent phase in the cycle of hair growth when the hair is retained in the hair follicle as a dead or "club" hair.

template   The single-stranded DNA blueprint for complementary strand assembly or the production of pre-mRNA.

terminal velocity   The maximum speed to which a free-falling drop of blood can accelerate in air which is approximately 25.1 feet per second.

test bullet   A bullet fired into a bullet recovery system in a laboratory for comparison or analysis.

test cartridge case   A cartridge case obtained while test firing a firearm in a laboratory to be used for comparison or analysis.

test-firing   The term used to designate the actual firing of a firearm in a laboratory to obtain representative bullets and cartridge cases for comparison or analysis.

test mark   A striated or impressed toolmark produced by the suspect tool which is to be used in making a comparison with the evidence mark.

terpenes   Volatile hydrocarbons which are normal constituents of wood.

thenar zone   The thick part of the palm on the radial (thumb) side of the hand.

THC (tetrahydrocannabinol)   The most active of the principle constituents of marijuana, and is contained in various parts of the plant.

thermal conductivity detector   A type of gas chromatographic detector which is sensitive to the change in the ability of the gases emerging from the column to conduct heat. A thermal conductivity (TC) detector is not as sensitive as a flame ionization detector, but it is capable of detecting some molecules, such as water, which give no signal on FID.

thermocycler A instrument that is programmed to heat and cool automatically. It is used to carry out the PCR steps.

thermolabile Decomposed, destroyed, affected, or liable to be adversely affected by heat, as some enzyme and toxins.

thermoplastic fiber A synthetic fiber that will soften or melt at high temperatures and harden again when cooled.

Thermus aquaticus (Taq). A bacterium that lives in hot springs.

thickness (T) The optical path through the fiber used for the calculation of birefringence, typically measured in micrometers.

thin-layer chromatography (TLC) A procedure for separating compounds by spotting them on a glass plate coated with a thin (about 0.01 inch) layer of silica or alumina, and "developing" the plate by allowing a solvent to move upward by capillary action. TLC is especially useful for identifying and comparing materials which are highly colored or which fluoresce under ultraviolet light. TLC is used extensively in explosive analysis and in the comparison of gasoline dyes, inks and various drugs.

thymine (T) One of the bases present in DNA, will only combine with adenine (A).

time exposure A comparatively long exposure made in seconds or minutes.

titer   The concentration in a solution of a dissolved substance as shown in titration. The least amount or volume needed to give a desired result in titration.

titrate   To make a series of dilutions.

titration   A method of analyzing the composition of a solution by adding known amounts of a standardized solution until a given reaction (color change, precipitation, or conductivitychange) is produced.

TLC   Thin-layer chromatography.

TMB   Tetramethylbenzidine

TNT (trinitrotoluene)   A high explosive used as a component of some priming mixtures.

toluene (methylbenzene)   An aromatic compound having the formula $C_6H_5CH_3$. A major component of gasoline. Toluene has a flash point of 40°F and explosive limits of 1.2% to 7%.

toolmark identification   Is a discipline of forensic science which has as its primary concern to determine if a toolmark was produced by a particular tool.

toxicity   The ability of a substance to cause injury to living tissue once it reaches a susceptible site in or on the body. The quality of being toxic.

toxicology   The study of poisons, including their nature, effects, and detection, and method of treatment.

trace forgery   Any fraudulent signature executed by actually following the outline of a genuine signature with a writing instrument. Such a signature may be produced with the aid of carbon paper by first tracing a carbon outline and then covering this with a suitable ink stroke, or the forgery may be traced from an outline made visible by light coming through the model signature and the fraudulent document.

trajectory The path described by an object or body moving in space. The path of a projectile after leaving the muzzle of a gun.

transfer pattern A contact bloodstain created when a wet, bloody surface contacts a second surface. A recognizable mirror image or at least a recognizable portion of the original surface may be transferred to the second surface.

transmittance (T) The ratio of radiant power transmitted by the sample: I, to the radiant power incident on the sample, I $T = I/I$

transmitted-light examination An examination in which the document is viewed withthe source of illumination behind it and the light passing through the paper.

transparency A positive photographic image on film, viewed or projected by transmitted light (light shining through film).

transitory defect An identifying typewriter characteristic that can be eliminated by cleaning the machine or replacing the ribbon. Clogged typeface are the most common defects of this class.

transverse waves Waves that vibrate in a sideways or transverse direction perpendicular to the direction in which the waves are traveling.

tremor A writing weakness portrayed by irregular, shaky strokes.

triacetate fiber Generic name for a manufactured fiber in which the fiber-forming substance is cellulose acetate. Where not less than 92% of the hydroxyl groups are acetylated, the term triacetate may be used as a generic description of the fiber.

trilobate Having three lobes.

tungsten   Metallic element; atomic number 74; hard brittle, gray solid. Has high electrical conductivity. Used in high-speed tool steel; filaments for electric light bulbs; and as heating elements in furnaces and vacuum-metallizing equipment. Also known as *wolfram*.

tungsten light   Light from regular room lamp and ceiling fixtures, not fluorescent.

turpentine   **1.** Gum. The pitch obtained from living pine trees. A sticky viscous liquid. **2.** Oil; a volatile liquid obtained by steam distillation of gum turpentine, consisting mainly of pinene and diterpene. Turpentine is frequently identified in debris samples containing burned wood.

TWGDAM   Technical Working Group on DNA Analysis Methods.

TWGMAT   Technical Working Group for Materials Analysis.

twist (lay)   The direction of twist in yarns is indicated by the capital letters S and Z. Yarn has an S-twist if when it is held vertically, the spirals around its central axis slope in the same direction as the middle portion of the letter S, and Z-twist if they slope in the same direction as the middle portion of the letter Z.

type ball   A device containing all the typeface of some single element typewriters and which by rotation and tilting prints the type.

type element   The type ball or type wheel of a single-element typewriter.

typeface   The printing surface of the type block or type element. On the typebar machine the type block is attached an arm, known as the typebar.

typeface defect   Any peculiarity in typewriting resulting from actual damage to the typeface metal. It may be an actual break in the outline of the letter where the metal is chipped away, sometimes referred to as broken type, or a distorted outline of the letter because of bent or smashed typeface metal. The defect can be corrected only by replacing the type block or element.

type lines   Are the two innermost ridges which run parallel and then diverge and surround the pattern area.

type wheel   In modern use, a series of characters mounted on flexible arms around a circular core. The wheel rotates to position each type, which is printed by a plunger striking against the back of the typeface forcing it against the ribbon and paper.

typing strip   A membrane containing immobilized DNA of known sequences.

twine   A strong string made up of two or more strands twisted together.

twist of rifling   Inclination of the spiral grooves (rifling) to the axis of the bore of a weapon; it is expressed as the number of calibers of length in which the rifling makes one complete turn.

twisted letter   Each character is designed to print at a certain fixed angle to the base line. Wear and damage to the type bars and the type block may cause some letters to become twisted so that they lean to the right or left of their correct slant.

U

Ulex Europeus seeds   Used in the preparation of anti-H lectin, which reacts strongly with the H-substances present in blood group O.

ultrasonic cleaner   An instrument used to clean objects submerged in a detergent or other solution by agitation from high frequency sound waves.

ultraviolet   Radiation in the region of the electromagnetic spectrum including wavelengths from 100 to 3,900.

ultraviolet examination   Ultraviolet radiation is invisible and occurs in the wavelengths just below the visible blue-violet end of the spectrum. The invisible rays react on some substances so that visible light is emitted, a phenomenon known as ultraviolet fluorescence. Thus, ultraviolet examination may be made visually or photographically by recording either the reflected ultraviolet or visible radiation.

ultraviolet light   Light rays beyond the visible spectrum of light at its violet end with wavelengths longer than X-rays, but shorter than visible light.

ultraviolet photograph   Any photograph that records the document under ultraviolet illumination. With some of these the ultraviolet radiation strikes the film, but with others a filter is employed so that the only visual fluorescence caused by the ultraviolet is recorded.

ultraviolet spectrometer   A device which produces a spectrum of ultraviolet light and is provided with a calibrated scale for measurement of wavelength.

underexposure A condition in which too little light reaches the film, producing a thin negative, a dark slide, or a muddy-looking print.

uniaxial With one axis; movement only in one plane, as of hinge-joint.

uracil The pyrimidine base in RNA that appears in place of the thymine found in DNA.

urea Is a protein denaturant, urea is qualified for use as the denaturing component in polyacrylamide gels.

UV transilluminator A source of ultraviolet (UV) light used to detect ethidium bromide stained DNA.

V

van der Waal's forces   Weak attractive forces acting between molecules. They are involved in the van der Waals equation of state for gases which compensates for the actual volume of the molecules and the forces acting between them.

vanillin   The methyl ether of protocatechuic aldehyde. It occurs in vanilla bean extract and in many balsams and resins.

vapor   A gas at a temperature below the critical temperature, so that it can be liquefied by compression, without lowering the temperature.

vaporization   The physical change of going from a solid or a liquid into a gaseous status.

variable   A property that may have different values in various cases.

variable number of tandem repeats (VNTR)   The variable number of repeat core base pair sequences at specific loci in the genome. The variation in length of the alleles formed from the repeats provides the basis for unique individual identification.

variable region   A region in an immunoglobin molecule that shows many sequence differences between antibodies of different specificities; the part of the antibody that binds to the antigen.

variance   A measure of the variation around the central class of a distribution; the average squared deviation of the observation from their mean value.

variant   Different type, usually applied to the rarer form.

vector   A self-replicating DNA molecule capable of transferring foreign DNA into a cell. For example, the human insulin gene can be cloned into the plasmid vector pB322 which in turn will replicate in *E. coli* cultures.

velocity   The speed of a projectile at a given point along its trajectory.

velocity, striking   The speed of a projectile upon impact.

velvet   A fabric with a short, thick-set pile of silk, cotton, or other fiber on a back that is closely woven and of the same or different fibers.

Vernier caliper   A measuring instrument having a fixed jaw and a sliding jaw with an attached vernier (short scale).

vertical malalignment   The result of a character printing above or below its proper position.

viscosity   The internal resistance to flow exhibited by a fluid.

visible print   Are made by fingers stained with colored materials, such as blood, ink, paint, grease, or dirt. Ordinarily, a visible print does not require further treatment to be fullyvisualized.

volatile   Prone to rapid evaporation. Both combustible and noncombustible materials may be volatile.

volumetric flask   A laboratory flask primarily intended for the preparation of definite, fixed volumes of solutions.

VSC#1   Video spectral comparator #1.

W

wad, base   A cylindrical component that is assembled into the head end of a shotshell.

wad, shot protector   Various designs of shot cups made of plastic and designed to reduce pellet deformation during barrel travel.

Wagner's reagent   An aqueous solution of iodine and potassium iodide; used for microchemical analysis of alkaloids. Also known as *Wagner's solution*.

wale   A column of loops lying lengthwise in a knit fabric.

Walker test   The original chemical test for the detection of the spatial distribution of nitrites in gunpowder residue.

warp   The set of yarn in all woven fabrics that runs lengthwise and parallel to the selvage and is interwoven with the filling.

wash   The process of removing nonbound or loosely bound probe from the blots after hybridization. This process reduces background interference.

watermark   A translucent design impressed in certain papers during the course of their manufacture. This is accomplished by passing a wet mat of fibers across a dandy roll, which is a metal cylinder containing patches of specific pattern designs. The design patches are generally of two types — wire or screen.

Watson & Crick model   Refers to the DNA molecule that forms a double-helix ladder with the complementary strands held by hydrogen bonds between specific bases pairs.

wave, castoff   A small blood droplet that originates from a parent drop of blood due to the wavelike action of the liquid in conjunction with striking a surface at an angle less than 90 degrees.

wavelength   The distance, measured along the line of propagation, between two points that are in phase on adjacent waves.

wave number   The number of wave per unit length, in a vacuum, usually given in reciprocal centimeters, cm^1.

wave theory   Radiation can be thought of as consisting of waves moving through space which transfer energy between non-connecting systems. The sun gives off light and heat and causes sunburn. Each of these effects is caused by electromagnetic radiation of different wavelengths (or frequencies).

weft (filling)   In a woven fabric, the yarn running from selvage to selvage at right angles to the wrap.

wide-angle lens   A lens that has a shorter focal length and a wider field of view (includes more subject area) than a normal lens.

Winchester-Western   A firearms manufacturer.

wipe   A bloodstain pattern created when an object moves through an existing bloodstain removing blood from the original stain and altering its appearance.

wipe test   A radioactivity contamination test whereby an ethanol wetted filter paper is wiped over the test area and the radioactivity determined. This test can also be used for the detection of DNA, by moisten cotton swab with distilled water and swabbing the work area where DNA has been extracted from forensic evidence.

word processing unit   Any typewriter or other printing unit that is combined with a memory system and is thus capable of automatic typewriting or repetitive typewriting of certain matter. Material can be stored on disks, tapes, or memory chips.

woven fabric   Generally used to refer to fabric composed of two sets of yarns, warp and weft (filling), that is formed by weaving, which is the interlacing of these sets of yarns.

writing condition   Both the circumstances under which the writing was prepared and the factors influencing the writer's ability to write at the time of execution. Circumstances pertaining to preparation involving the writer's position (sitting, standing, bedridden, etc.), the paper support and backing, and the writing instrument; writing ability may be modified by the condition of the writer's health, nervous state, or degree of intoxication.

writing impression   The small writing indentation completely or virtually devoid of any pigment. It may be made on the sheet of tablet paper that was immediately below the one on which writing was done or remain after pencil or typewriting has been thoroughly erased.

writing ink   A solution of colorant in water, usually containing also low percentages of tannic or gallic acid. Fountain pen inks retain the fluidity of water; for ballpoint pens the mixture is of a paste-like consistency.

writing offset   The result of a paper coming in contact with fresh ink writing. It may be the mirror image of entire words or sentences, as are sometimes found on a blotter, or merely fragments of words or letters.

wrong-handed writing   Any writing executed with the opposite hand from that normally used. Often referred to this writing as "with the awkward hand." It is a means of disguise. Thus, the writing of a right-handed person written with his left-hand accounts for the common terminology for this class of disguise as "left-handed writing."

X

Xerox™　A positive photocopy made directly on plain paper. Although Xerox is a trade name, its success, like Photostat's before it, has resulted in many people referring incorrectly to all present-day photocopies as xeroxes.

X-chromosome　A chromosome responsible for sex determination. Two copies are present in the genome of the homogametic sex and one copy in the heterogametic sex. The human female has two X-chromosomes and the male has one X.

X-linked　Genes on the X-chromosome.

X-ray　Electromagnetic radiation of shorter wavelength than visible light that is capable of penetrating solids.

X-ray diffraction　An analytical technique used to identify crystalline solids by measuring the characteristic spaces between layers of atoms or molecules in a crystal. X-ray diffraction can be very useful in the identification of explosive residue.

X-ray fluorescence emission spectrometer　An X-ray crystal spectrometer used to measure wavelengths of X-ray fluorescence; in order to concentrate beams of low intensity, it has bent reflecting or transmitting crystals arranged so that the theoretical curvature required can be varied with the diffraction angle of a spectrum line.

xylene dimethylbenzene　A commercial mixture of the three isomers, ortho-, meta-, and paraxylene. The last two predominate. Used as protective coatings; solvent for alkyd resins, lacquers, rubber cements; synthesis of organic chemicals. An aromatic compound having the formula $C_6H_4(CH_3)_2$. Xylene is a major component of gasoline. A mixture of toluene and xylene if frequently used as automotive paint thinner. The flash points of these isomers range from 81 to 115°F. Para xylene, with a flash point of 81°F, is used to calibrate flash point testers. The explosive limits of xylene are 1.0% to 7.0%.

Y

Y- chromosome   A chromosome responsible for sex determination in the heterogametic sex. This occurs in male (XY) mammals.

yaw   The angle between the longitudinal axis of a projectile and a line tangent to the trajectory at the center of gravity of the projectile.

yield gel   The mobility of the undigested DNA indicates the quality of the isolated DNA. Undigested DNA is applied to a 15-cm agarose gel, size separated by electrophoresis and stained with ethidium bromide. This gel is to aid in assessing the amount of total DNA recovered from a sample, as well as the state of degradation of the DNA.

Z

zoom lens A lens in which the focal length can be adjusted over a wide range, giving the photographer, in effect, lenses of many focal lengths.

zwilling European term for a double-barreled shoulder arm with one rifled and one smooth-bored barrel.

Z-twist A right-handed yarn twist in which the spiral slants like the middle part of the letter Z.

zygosity Twin development from on or two zygotes. If one, the twins are identical (monozygotic); if two, they are fraternal (dizygotic).

zygote The product of the union of two gametes.

Bibliography

Kirby, L. T., *DNA Fingerprint An Introduction*, W. H. Freeman and Company, New York, 1992.

AFTE Standardization Committee, *Glossary of the Association of Firearms and Toolmark Examiners*, Fonville Printing Company 1980.

Lewin, B., *Genes V*, Oxford University Press Inc., New York, 1994.

Saferstein, R., *Forensic Science Handbook*, Prentice Hall Inc., 1982, Englewood Cliff, N.J..

Garrett, R. H., and Grisham, C. M., *Biochemistry*, Saunders College Publishing 1995.

Sheindlin, Judge G., and Whitney, C. , *Blood Trail*, Ballantine Books, New York, 1996.

Hilton, O., *Scientific Examination of Questioned Documents*, Elsevier North Holland Inc., New York, New York 1982.

Griffiths, A.J.F., Miller, J. H., Suzuki, D. T., Lewontin, R. C. and Gelbart, W.M., *An Introduction to Genetic Analysis*, W.H. Freeman and Company 1993.

Technical Working Group on DNA Analysis Method, 1995, *Guideline for a Quality Assurance Program for DNA Analysis*, Crime Laboratory Digest Vol. 22, Number 2, pages 21-43.

Griffin, H.G., and Griffin, A.M., *PRC Technology Current Innovations*, CRC Press Inc. 1994.

McGraw-Hill, *Dictionary of Scientific and Technical Terms*, McGraw-Hill Inc. 1974.

American Society for Testing and Materials, *Standard Definitions of Terms Relating to Glass Products*, ASTM Standards (Philadelphia, Pa.: ASTM, 1965) Part 13, p.145.

Cowger, J. F., *Friction Ridge Skin Comparison and Identification of Fingerprints*, CRC Press Inc. 1993.

Cowger, J. F., *Friction Ridge Skin Comparison and Identification of Fingerprints*, CRC Press Inc. 1993.

Eckert, W. G, MD and James, S. H., *Interpretation of Bloodstain Evidence at Crime Scenes*, Elsevier Science Publishing Co. Inc., 1989.

Gardner, E. J.., Simmons, M.J. and Snustad, D. P., *Principles of Genetics*, John Wiley and Sons, Inc. 8th edition, 1991.

DeForest, P. R., Gaensslen, R. E., Lee, H. C., Forensic Science: An Introduction to Criminalistics, McGraw-Hill Companies, 1983.

Appendix:
Firearms Manufacturers

Rossi S.A. Metalurgica E
  Municoes
Rua Amadeo Rossi 143
Sao Leopoldo RS
Brazil 93 030
Phone: 0512-92-5566
(U.S. importer: Interarms)

Beretta U.S.A. Corporation
17601 Beretta Drive
Accokeek, MD 20607
Phone: 301-283-2191

Browning Arms Cormpany
Route 1
Morgan UT 84050
Phone: 801-876-2711
(General Offices)

Charter Arms Company
  (CHARCO)
26 Beaver Street.
Ansonia, CT 06401
Phone: 203-735-4686

CIL
Canadian Industries Limited
Imperial/Canuck
Montreal, Quebec, Canada

Clerke Company
P.O. Box 627
Peachblossom, CA 93553-
  0627
Phone: 805-945-0713
Fax: 201-440-4939

Colt Manufacturing Co.
P.O. Box 1868
Hartford, CT 06101
Phone: 203-236-6311
Fax: 713-433-6201

Federal Cartridge Company
900 Ehlen Drive
Anoka, MN 55303
Phone: 612-422-2840

Harrington & Richardson
  (H&R 1871 Inc.)
60 Industrial Row
Gardner, MA 01440
Phone: 508-632-9393
Fax: 508-632-2300

Israel Military Industries
  (IMI)
P.O. Box 1044
Ramat Hasharon 47100
Phone: 972-3-5485222

(IMI U.S. importers: Action Arms Ltd. KBI, Inc. Magnum Research, Inc. Springfield Armory)

Ithaca Gun Company/
Ithaca Aquisition Corp.
891 Route 34B
King's Ferry, NY 13081
Phone: 315-364-7171

Marlin Firearms Company
100 Kenna Drive
New Haven, CT 06473
Phone: 203-239-5621
Fax: 203-234-7991

Mossberg & Sons, Inc.
7 Grasso Avenue.
New Haven, CT 06473
Phone: 203-288-6491
Fax: 203-288-2404

Numrich Arms Corporation
203 Broadway
West Hurley, NY 12491

Remington Arms
Corporation
1007 Market Street
Wilmington, DE 19898
Phone: 302-773-5291

Savage Arms, Inc.
Springdale Road
Westfield, MA 01085
Phone: 413-586-7001

Smith & Wesson
2100 Roosevelt Ave..
Springfield, MA 01102
Phone: 413-781-8300

Sturm, Ruger & Co., Inc.
Lacey Place
Southport, CT 06490
Phone: 203-259-7843

Winchester-Western (U.S.
Repeating Arms Co., Inc.)
275 Winchester Avenue.
New Haven, CT 06511
Phone: 203-789-5000